ESSENTIALS OF

NETWORK

MARKETING

SUDESH RAVI MALIK

ISBN 979-8-88783-563-1

Dedicated to my brother

Late Updesh Malik

A hardcore networker

Welcome

So you have decided to join the wagon to riches. The network marketing industry is the fastest growing business in the world today that allows you to have the potential to create wealth for yourself.

UNBREAKABLE ★ UNSHAKEABLE
BELIEVE
IN
YOURSELF
DARE
TO
DREAM
UNS

Direct Sale
$ 2.9 Bi

PREFACE

"**P**rospecting" for business as you've known it, has become obsolete. It's an irrelevant, old-school sales technology that only those who haven't learned the principles on which cosmic sponsoring is founded pursue.

I'd like you to stop and think for a moment. Compare today's social environment to the world we lived in 15 years ago.

Today, people are drowning in a flood of information, marketing noise, and endless options to choose from thanks to the internet.

Corporations have effectively reduced us to numbers, tracked our buying habits, categorized our topics of interest, and constantly use that information to drive as many customized offers into our viewing screen. People have been forced to build fortified walls around themselves and their homes to fight back the onslaught of people trying to get their hands into their pocketbook.

Unfortunately, 95% of those who start a home business will fail themselves, and the primary reason for that failure is their lack of knowledge and skills necessary to succeed in today's modern, competitive marketplace. You have two options when it comes to building your business:

- You can simply play the numbers and contact enough people until you make a sale through traditional, old-school prospecting and this is the path 95% of home business owners take.

- You can position yourself in the marketplace in a manner that allows interested prospects to find you, and contact you.

Option #2 is obviously the superior choice for several reasons, but I'd like to point out one dynamic that is key to the concept of Miracle Sponsorship.

Who finds and contacts the other person first is very important. In Option 1, you were chasing the prospect. In Option 2, the prospect was chasing you, which means you are perceived as the expert and hold all of the power and value in that situation.

The prospect invited you into his world and is basically asking you to sell him your goods or services. You get to instantly bypass all of the barriers that must be broken down by everyone else, and suddenly this won't be about selling anymore.

You'll then be in the position of a knowledgeable service provider whose expertise has been sought out and pursued.

This is where you have to be today to break through the infinite noise in today's marketplace.

How do you do this?

Simple. Unlike business prospects, there is only one of you in the entire globe which makes you the most effective marketing tool you have.

What we teach in Miracle Sponsoring is how to use marketing strategies to become that person, that leader, and that expert that everyone wants to work with. The type of person whose phone calls and emails are welcomed and valued instead of detested and deleted.

You can be that person.

I've been studying human psychology for several years now, and what might surprise you, is that attraction between people isn't really a choice, it's a biological response.

By learning to control these attraction switches within ourselves, we automatically begin to attract others. Two of the most powerful triggers in existence are value and status. People are genetically programmed to feel attraction toward others who have equal or higher levels of value and status and you're no different. We respond this way because we stand to gain power through the association with that person. If you can establish a relationship with a person of greater status and value, your value and status automatically increase as well through that association alone.

- New doors and opportunities are opened.
- You can learn new, inside information that is only available to others in that circle.
- New alliances and partnerships with other powerful people can be formed.
- This is why you're on training calls every week to gain insights from a successful team leader.

This is why you idolize the top distributors on stage at your company events and crowd around them to listen in to their conversations. This is why your stand and cheer for your company's CEO when he speaks. These people have something of value to offer you, and by associating with them, you gain power.

I used to think that sponsoring was just about numbers. That it was about scripts and saying the right words. But no matter what I did, I struggled to build a team of distributors for years, until I realized the difference between myself, and the leaders in my company who were sponsoring dozens of new reps every month, they were different because they held value in the eyes of their prospects and they knew how to convey that value in their marketing.

Their prospects saw this, and they were attracted to these individuals. They wanted to work with them and it was a privilege to be sponsored by them because they knew that there was power and knowledge to be gained in such a relationship.

So where does that leave you?

If you're not sponsoring new distributors, if prospects don't return your phone calls, or respond to your emails, it's because you don't hold any value in their eyes. You have nothing to offer them.

And that's ok. Everyone starts from square one, but if you want to achieve the highest levels of success in this industry, you need to change that.

The best way to increase your value is to increase your knowledge. Spend a good year buying/attending every course and seminar you can on Multi-Level Marketing (MLM) industry, marketing, copyrighting, and personal development, and by the end of that year, you would have so much to offer to your prospects, that sponsoring literally would become effortless.

SUDESH MALIK

Sudesh Malik has graduated from Mastery University of Tony Robbins (international speaker and author, honored as one of the ten "outstanding People of the World" in 1977)

Sudesh Malik got into MLM in 1995 much before most MLM companies had started their business in India. In 1996, he was part of a UK-based company operating in India. In 1999, along with a UK-based team he was the founder Director of Cymbionic Mkt. Pvt. Ltd. along with the UK-based team. He was active in the industry until 2002, when he decided to explore the hospitality sector before taking a position as brand manager for a UAE-based organization having operations in 40 countries. He further ventured into corporate and documentary filmmaking and finally, after a break of approximately 14 years, returned to network marketing and repeated his previous success once again with his huge and successful team.

Sudesh Malik has trained thousands of sales executives/MLM professionals and lakhs of ambitious individuals have attended and appreciated his seminars all over the country. He lives by the words of Zig Ziglar—

"Help enough people to get what they want and you will get what you want in life."

Remember,
in Network Marketing industry,
we grow by helping others where as in
corporate world many grow by pushing others out

THANK YOU

This book and my work in the Network Marketing industry would be incomplete without the dedication and support of my Miracle Team members from all over India. Your passion for the mission has brought you all from different walks of life to dedicate your time, energy, and efforts to help others experience the rewards of network marketing and realize their aspirations. I extend my deepest and most sincere gratitude to each and every one of you for all that you do. Thank you for being a part of this journey. I look forward to journeying even further with you.

My special thanks to

* Satpal Sagar, *Delhi*
* Daulat Tungaria, *Mumbai*
* Tarun Advani, *Mumbai*
* Deepak Bambani, *Mumbai*
* Akant Pathak, *Bhopal*
* Dr. Acharya, *Kolkatta*
* Dyneshwar Dorkar, *Nagpur*
* Manoj Tiwari, *Indore*
* Preeti Kukkar, *Chandigarh*
* Om Prakash, Sikkar

* Mahesh Hada, *Indore*
* Santosh Mahanti, *Dantewada*
* Deepak Singh, *Patna*
* Y K Pradhan, *Raipur*
* Rashmi Pradhan, *Bhubaneshwar*
* Pratyush Mahakul, *Cuttack*
* Arun Gupta, *Delhi*
* Prempal Singh, *Agra*
* Harish Kumar, *Jaipur*

Once again, thank you for being part of our mission of spreading financial freedom in the easiest and in most natural way, by word of mouth.

CONTENTS

01 INTRODUCTION TO MULTI-LEVEL MARKETING

Network Marketing, also known as Multi-Level Marketing (MLM) is a strategy in which we spend no capital, just time. Network marketing business has produced the most number of millionaires worldwide. The future of the industry in the 21st century is network marketing. It has grown rightly over time. Today, direct sales have a strong tendency for developing career chances that start as part-time jobs. It has arisen as a viable income source and commercial marketing success in the last five years. In recent years, Network Marketing has significantly increased in India.

The global economy was shaken by the recent COVID-19 pandemic which has made network marketing vital in spurring growth. During the pandemic, multiple businesses were disrupted and lakhs of people lost their jobs in a short time. This has caused an increasing number of young entrepreneurs to switch their careers and venture into Network Marketing.

Network marketing is a type of direct selling where you are rewarded for building your own sales team. This can be done by either selling products or services to customers or by recruiting other people to join your team who subsequently earn by selling the product or services and get a small percentage on their sales too. The MLM company pays you commissions and bonuses based on your and your team's sales.

Network marketing business is made up of three parts:

1) Distribution of products and services

2) The compensation plan

3) The company (Three P's—Product, Plan, and People)

Instead of relying on retail outlets, in network marketing, products and services are distributed via direct consumers. In fact, if you are involved in any network marketing company which is distributing their products/services using additional channels, you should seriously reconsider your options.

Your success in network marketing business depends on the confluence of the right team and the right company. You might be wondering why we left products and compensation plans out of the equation. Well, that's because a 'right' company and a 'right' team will solve all your concerns.

Now, how to tell which company is good or right for **you**?

1.1   Is Network Marketing/MLM Right for You?

Because multi-level marketing plans are commission-based. The participants do not receive salaries. That means, MLM businesses are often best suited for people with an entrepreneurial spirit, who can set their own goals and schedules, who are good at sales, and who can effectively network with others not only to sell products but to recruit new marketers.

1.2   India and Network Marketing

It won't be out of turn to say that today the Indian economy is one of the most important places for economic development, and the entire globe is closely observing its expansion. Hence India is one of the most sought-after destinations for investments and business opportunities.

Talking of Network Marketing in India, the country has experienced slow but rather reasonably steady growth in this context. Early players like Amway India, Modicare, and Oriflame India introduced the concept of direct selling and MLM to the people of this country. Today, there are only a few people who have never heard of popular brands like Amway or Oriflame which says that the direct selling industry has therefore gained at least a minimum level of footage in the country.

Network Marketing in the present Indian context

In India, MLM organizations are still new and not many organized companies exist. But as more companies enter the space and begin to utilize technology, their network will expand rapidly and so would the industry.

Network marketing is growing at a rapid pace in India and it is estimated to reach Rs. 15,930 crores by the end of 2021. The latest FICCI-KPMG survey shows that by 2025, retail sales could cross Rs. 64,500 crores and provide 1.8 crore Indians, that include 60% women, self-employment, Industry experts estimate that this number is significantly higher when you include people who work in unorganized sectors.

The direct sales industry in India is looking very promising considering its earnings (which are reaching new heights). The network marketing industry in India is just starting to get exciting, and there are tremendous prospects for it. Various government schemes such as Digital India and Make in India are aimed at increasing online presence. The Indian direct sales industry has been doing well lately, with higher earnings predicted in the near future. Network marketing appeals to people because it provides,

1. Better youth employment in times of bad job security because of economic instability.

2. Source of a second income

3. Women empowerment

4. Opportunities for passive income

5. able to live a luxury life and be financially free

6. Contribution to society

7. Job enhancement

8. SME opportunities

The Indian MLM industry is witnessing, a tide of MLM and direct selling firms operating in the market. A large portion of this tide consists of unorganized small players who are not serious about the MLM business and portray it as a "get rich overnight" opportunity. With this, the image of the industry in India has been tarnished. Many people now see MLM as a scheme run by fraudulent fly-by-night companies. This perception is also true, given that innumerable unorganized and small MLM companies have flown away and vanished from the market after collecting subscription or joining fees from thousands of customers. The amount goes up to millions of rupees.

The other side of this story should also be given proper attention. Today, finding quality from a vast quantity has become a norm. In India, hordes of companies are going the direct selling or MLM way. Many of these are good and legitimate companies and many are not, it is from these numerous companies and firms that the potentially good firms would carve a niche for them. The entry of numerous firms in the industry shows its potential recognition and it is from among these companies that many emerge as well-performing and profitable entities.

Challenges before the Indian MLM industry today

- To familiarize and educate people about the concepts such as Direct Selling and Network Marketing/MLM

- To build a perceptual appreciation of MLM in the minds of people

- To positively portray MLM and Direct Selling as a means of

- marketing and distribution rather than as a "get rich overnight" opportunity.

- To explore the employment potential of MLM by involving more and more people into Direct Selling as Independent Direct Sellers.

- Ensuring the least failure of direct sellers by imparting proper training and development programs.

- To lobby with industry associations like FICCI (Federation of Indian Chambers for Commerce and Industry) and CII (Confederation of Indian Industries) for better networking and industry support and recognition.

- To maintain a common code of ethics.

- To identify and stop fraudulent, fly-by-night firms endorsing MLM business as a "get rich opportunity" in India.

- To coordinate with the Government of India to come up with a comprehensive set of policies and rules for the Direct Selling industry in form of a Direct Selling Act.

- To encourage reputed and established business players in India to venture into MLM/Direct Selling, portraying the same as a viable and profitable futuristic business opportunity cum means of sales and distribution.

Threats before India's Direct Selling Industry

- Unrestricted entry of small mushrooming players into the industry

- Ignorance about direct selling on part of people

- Growing acceptance of direct selling by people as a fraudulent and misleading business

- Lack of knowledge on MLM resulting from improper/inadequate education and training.

- Lack of government's interest in the industry and absence of proper legislative enactment/rules for the regulation of the industry.

1.3   How Network Marketing is perceived in India

When we talk about network marketing, first we visualize going door to door, selling shampoos, and so on. Not that there is anything wrong with that, but that is, unfortunately, the common perception about this industry.

Changing the name from direct selling to Multi-Level Marketing (MLM), and then to network marketing may help correct the picture in the long run but it will not change its perception overnight.

So, what exactly is network marketing? This industry, in our opinion, develops into whatever you decide it to be. If you see this as a purely sales business, inevitably you will sell lots and this works well for many people!

If some see it as a get-rich-quick scheme, they will probably play that game and might do well, too. Your values determine your habits and your understanding determines your actions. invariably, these will determine how this business is done by you.

We choose to see network marketing as a paradigm shift in terms of how products are distributed to consumers, bypassing the middleman in the traditional channels by going directly to the consumers. We choose to see network marketing as building a network of consumers getting unique and better-quality products at a reasonable price.

We choose to see this industry as an opportunity to shift wealth from the hands of giant conglomerates to the man on the street. We choose to believe that this industry will build a long-term asset that will provide players with a residual and passive income for a long time to come.

Network marketing, in its simplest form, is about sharing with others information about a product or service that you love, thus, setting into motion the process of word-of-mouth advertising and increasing customer outreach manifold.

Are the promises of network marketing all a dream or are they for real? Well, it is real enough for us. But like any other dream, it remains as unattainable for most people because they don't put enough effort into it to make it come true. A decent amount of focus and discipline is essential to reap its benefits.

When we first considered the offer, we evaluated it just like any other business we were running at the time. The ability of this firm to let us leverage our time to make riches may have been the most appealing factor that attracted us to it. What if we stop working tomorrow? Network marketing is, to us, the greatest opportunity that will allow us to build an asset that will continue to look after us financially, even if we stop working tomorrow.

There are, of course, a number of conditions needed in order to enable this. The most important of which is choosing the right company. It is also the greatest opportunity as it allows us to build a global business. This industry lends itself to that possibility because of the increasing internationalization of numerous network marketing companies. This business is relatively easy to take to another country as long as your company is also there.

For many others in this industry, it is the greatest opportunity, simply because entering this business is easy and the growth prospects are immense.

Where do we expect this industry to head? As we have told many of our distributors, if you do not recruit your uncles, aunts, nephews, nieces, or friends and colleagues into the business, someone else will. This industry will boom without any doubt. While we say that, we also point out that the industry is going through tremendous changes. Unless veteran network marketers change with the times, they might end up like the dinosaurs of the past.

Two forces are pushing this change. First, the increasing influence of technology as an enabler in this industry; and second, the changing demographics of people that are entering this industry. Network marketers can be left behind if they don't keep up with new technologies and update both their systems and their methods.

The past does not equal the future and the future is vibrant and exciting. If you are with us, enter this new frontier with confidence and enthusiasm. If you are not yet in' our industry, get out of your box and do something different. Who knows, you might find your life back!

1.4 Types of Compensation Plans

Never base your decision to choose one network marketing organization over another just on the compensation plan. Your decision should be based on your research. However, before you join any network marketing company, it is still imperative that you have a thorough understanding of how your preferred MLM company's compensation plan works. This effort is well worth it considering that you will want to stick with the same company in the long term. It is always better to do your research early and make the right choice than to hop from one MLM company to another when you discover the compensation plan does not work well for you even though you had other reasons to select the company earlier. Your reputation in this industry is important as MLM is a relationship business and credibility is an important asset. In addition to that, you will also not want to be labeled as an "MLM Junkie" by others.

There are many types of compensation plans out there. The most common ones are the four listed below:

1. Stairstep-Breakaway

2. Matrix

3. Board

4. Unilevel

5. Binary

6. Australian 2-Up (In India, it is also called Australian binary)

7. Generation plan

8. Monoline/Single line plan

9. Gift plan

10. Point plan

Stairstep-Breakaway

The Stairstep-Breakaway plan, as the name suggests, is a combination of two plans: The Stairstep and the Breakaway plan. Let's look at both these plans individually.

a) Stairstep Plan

The Stairstep Plan is the compensation plan that pays you for the total volume of your group. The total volume of your group can be achieved by your personal sales volume or your downlines' sales volume.

Say, you are a director, and you have one manager, one supervisor, and one associate directly below you. If all of you achieved 100 personal sales volume in a particular month, you will receive a 20% rebate on your personal sales volume, 5% overriding commission from your manager, 10% overriding commission from your supervisor and 15% overriding commission from your associate in that particular month. In summary, you will receive an overriding commission based on the difference in your rank and the rank of those that you have sponsored.

b) The Breakaway Plan

In the Breakaway Plan, when someone you directly sponsored in your personal group achieved a certain rank (often called the Director), they will "breakaway" from your personal group and take away both the distributors and volume that are underneath them from you. They are now considered one of your first-generation breakaway groups. You will then earn a monthly overriding commission on the volume produced by this entire group by meeting the plan's monthly defined personal group sales volume requirement. With most breakaway plans, the more first-generation breakaway groups you have, the more generations deep of breakaways you will be qualified to be paid on. In this way, it gives people incentive to keep building. General comments about the Stairstep-Breakaway plans are:

1. Once the person that you sponsored "breaks away", you will need to get other people to fill the gap to achieve your personal sales volume in order to meet the plan's monthly requirement. As such, this plan may not be suitable for part-timers.

2. The plan is more suitable for full-timers as compared to part-timers and generally rewards heavy-hitters better than the part-timers. Those who are able to make it will be able to earn big money, while those who do it on a part-time basis have a high tendency to drop out. The key to success for this plan is to have a balanced and fair compensation plan that will provide enough incentive to the "heavy hitters" as well as not discourage the part-timers.

Matrix

The unique characteristic of the Matrix Plan is in its limited width. The Matrix limits the number of direct distributors you can sponsor to usually less than five people. Take for example, a 3x3 Matrix means you can sponsor only three people on your first level and you can get paid for overriding commissions on group sales volume produced by three levels deep of distributors. In this example, you can have a maximum of three direct distributors (first level), a maximum of nine second-level distributors, and a maximum of 27 third-level distributors.

There are many other variations of the Matrix. For example:

The 2x12 Matrix, the 3x5 Matrix, the 3x7 Matrix. But the concept is similar, that is, the first number refers to the number of direct sponsors you can have and the second number refers to the number of levels that you can get overriding commissions on the group volume.

Understand the Matrix plans better

A. Spill-over will benefit the part-timers who did not work too hard but have strong sponsors as their sponsors have no choice but to put it below them since the number of direct sponsors in the Matrix plan has a width limitation. However, if you are a heavy-hitter, and you have many 'do-nothing distributors' on you first level, it may dramatically hurt your earnings depending on the percentage of commission that you are given out at each level of the matrix.

B. It is important to know how many levels the commission is being paid at, as well as the percentage of payout for each level of the matrix. Some matrix plans may be designed to pay a bigger percentage of the commissions at more distant levels to encourage the heavy hitters to stay on with the company. Deeper the levels, more the people. This may not be favorable to part-timers.

Board Plan

The Board plan MLM is also known as the 'Revolving Matrix Plan' and it has a limited number of people. As the name suggests, a board constitutes the centerpiece in this plan. It has a few distributors on it depending on the type of board plan in usage.

The commonly adopted board plan is a 2×2 board plan wherein each member has to recruit two other people. This continues till all the positions on the board are filled. When the number of members exceeds the limit of the board, it is split into two sub-boards and the top member is promoted to the higher level. This keeps repeating every time a board reaches the maximum allowed members.

Unilevel

Unilevel literally means one level. This is definitely not what Unilevel is all about since most companies using the Unilevel type compensation plan usually pay a few levels deep. Depending on the maximum number of levels deep (n) that commissions are being paid.

So, distributors can recruit as many people as their direct downlines as possible or at the first level but the group commissions payouts are capped by the finite depth that the plan allows. If the plan pays up to five levels deep, then you will not be able to earn any commissions from anyone on your sixth level and beyond. In this plan, there is also no breakaway. So, technically speaking, this means that a traditional Breakaway plan will generally pay down many more levels of distributors than the standard Unilevel plan can and should.

General comments about the Unilevel plans:

1. Unilevel plan is a simple plan that is easy to understand. In the beginning, distributors like them because they can get paid commissions quickly. However, they may become discouraged when their organization starts to grow bigger, especially at the deeper levels where they could not get any overriding commissions. This may cause the heavy hitters to move to another company that pays more aggressively to the heavy hitters.

2. If you are a leader and you are working directly with the heavy hitter on your fifth level, you will not stand to gain much from his first level recruits and beyond because the four levels in between (who are basically consumers) will definitely not quit because they have so much easy money coming from the heavy hitter beneath them. They probably will not get rich but they can definitely make more money than the products that they need to consume in order to stay qualified each month. This prevents the volume from compressing up to the leaders (who are doing the real work).

Binary

The Binary plan as the name suggests is actually a 2xn matrix plan where 'n' is the number of levels where commissions can be derived from. In most Binary compensation plans, the 'n' is actually infinity. The distributors own what are called Income or Business Centers (BC). Each Business Center can recruit only two direct sponsors—one left leg and one right leg. Additional recruits will be added to the levels below the first level. This will not be a problem since most binary compensation plans pay commission based on the total group volume of each business center up to infinity level.

With one business center, as you sponsor distributors, you place them in the open positions in your downline, either on your left leg or right leg. The accumulated volume at both legs are compared on a weekly basis for commission payout calculations. The key to binary plans is to build organizations that are balanced.

Please also note that there is a maximum amount that can be carried forward as well as a maximum commission payout per week. The maximum amount that can be carried forward and the maximum commission payout per week is to ensure that the company does not pay above a certain level as commission payable since the binary plans normally extend to infinity level.

In some of the binary plans, once any business center is maximized, the distributor is allowed to re-enter his own downline with a new business center. This is to ensure that the earning potential of the distributors is not capped once their business centers are maximized.

Australian "TWO-UP"

This refers to a structure where the first two people you recruit are "given" to your sponsor and all the rest of the people you recruit are yours. Each person you recruit will in turn give you the first two people they recruit, keeping the rest for themselves. This does not create a matrix, but only something that resembles a front line. The front line keeps growing, as you recruit new people, and as the people you recruit give you their first two recruits.

In order to prevent people from strategically picking weak prospects to give to their upline, that is, by keeping strong prospects for themselves, there may also be an over-riding mechanism, wherein you get a bonus on whatever structure is built by the people you give to your upline.

Generation plan

Here, the business plan is based on profit-sharing while marketing business. It is also called as Gap Commission Plan or Repurchase Plan. Generation Plan MLM is a powerful MLM Plan which can pay up to many levels. All downline members or agents can be seen as distinct rates in this plan and this plan is generally based on the business model of revenue sharing in which income is distributed among all the participants according to the organizational business plan. This system is also known as 'Repurchase' or 'Generation Gap Policy' in certain specific areas.

MLM generation plan is a bit complicated to understand for ordinary people compared to other compensation plans. But this plan comes with other great features that make this plan acceptable and popular in network marketing. A member is paid up to several levels in this package, and the scope of the rates also provides a member with an added benefit of improving salesmanship and profits.

Monoline

The Monoline plan is widely known as the Single Line, or simple one-dimensional plan that holds one leg for each participant. You will not find any form of ceiling or capping in Monoline, and no required level of business. In the Monoline scheme, timing is the most important thing because this program is entirely based on first-come, first-serve basis. If you're joining early in the network, it would be highly profitable. You can earn money just by recruiting a single member. Even when your down-line members recruit someone, you get the profit.

Gift plan

This particular MLM plan also can be called 'Donation plan' or 'Help plan.' The policy is—give and take. When you join the network, you donate some money to your up-line. When people join under you, you get donations. You'll have to give one time, but you get a multiple or an unlimited number of times. This kind of MLM plan is banned in many countries as the governments of these countries view this plan as a money laundering scheme.

Point plan

In this plan, the company assigns certain points (usually six-eight) and each point has a value attached. On joining, a new agent is entitled for one point for his sale and the rest of the points are distributed amongst his up-line as per their ranks. On achieving a certain number of sales (direct or indirect) an agent is promoted to a higher rank, thus receiving more points for the sale, resulting in higher compensation.

You keep getting promoted on achieving certain accumulated sales—your sale plus team sales—till the time you achieve the highest rank, where you get the highest number of points which are to be compensated by the company. This means, the higher rank you achieve the higher are you paid for the same work that you have been doing. Plus, you are also compensated for the sales done by your downline.

In this compensation plan, the agent at the bottom gets paid first and the remaining points are distributed upwards. Once the maximum points to be distributed on a sale are allotted before it reaches a certain agent, that agent will not be paid or paid less for that particular sale as all the points or certain points were distributed before it reaches him. This happens when the structure goes deeper.

Most companies mix and match various plans to create a unique compensation plan for their distributors.

Four-Step Success System:

1. Master prospecting one-on-one, over the phone using a script.
2. Master closing one-on-one on phone using a script.
3. You must have your own live or recorded presentation on YouTube and other formats
4. You must master training others on step 1 and step 2

Category 1: The Bottle Rockets

These opportunities often experience an exponential growth curve. But of course, their downward trajectory is even more dramatic once they experience the regulator scrutiny that is inevitable for schemes like these.

It's important to understand that the opportunities in this category are **not** Network Marketing programs, even though they often claim otherwise. These would include chain letters, real estate plotting, money doubling schemes, gold schemes, currency schemes, magic gas/pill/pendants, and other schemes that are just excuses for people to move money to the top of the structure. They are illegal and they hurt people.

Category 2: The Old Guard

These are the companies that hit and actually sustained momentum for a significant period of time. They are now billion-dollar-plus companies and have already created legacy incomes for people who got in early and became a reason for their growth. These are fine companies offering stability and the chance for a steady income.

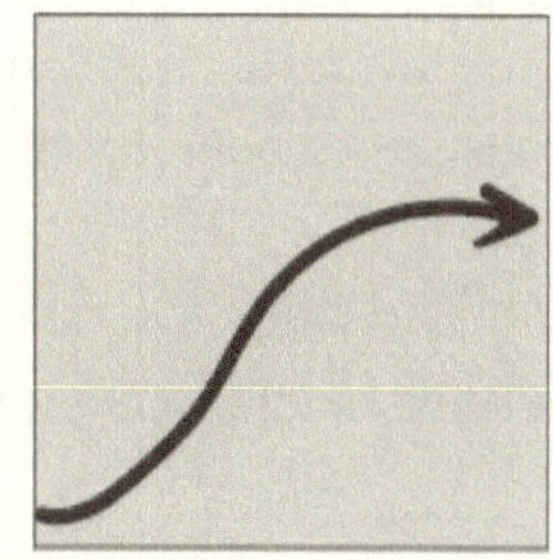

But most industry experts would agree that your chances of creating significant wealth with them have expired.

They have reached a level of maturity that prevents someone from starting with them today and creating large bonus checks or exponential growth.

Category 3: The Flat-Liners

These companies are the bridesmaids that never got to be the bride. They have been around for a long period of time, but never hit that curve of exponential growth. The only growth they have, if any, is incremental growth, usually coming from opening new markets. They have been operating for a long time and have failed to capture the imagination of the public. 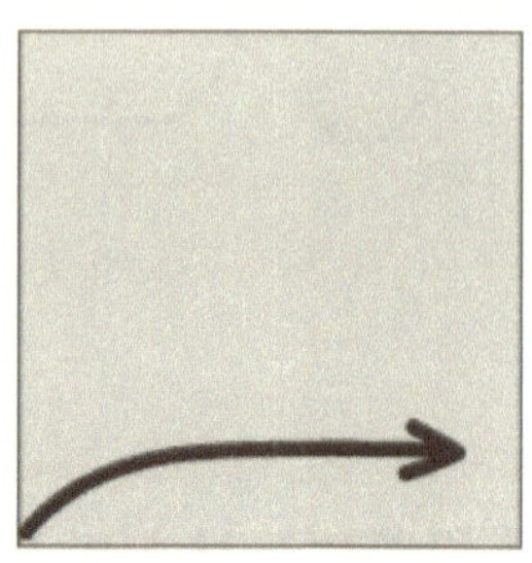

There are many reasons why these companies did not reach momentum. Often it is because their products are not viable, their compensation plan does not promote the correct behavior, or it is being driven by inexperienced individuals with poor management.

Of course, these companies often tout their longevity and suggest that momentum is imminent. But history has shown that the companies that reach momentum today do so in the early years. It's virtually impossible to create substantial wealth with a flat-line company unless you are willing to hang around for decades.

Category 4: The Peddlers

These programs probably create more misunderstandings and broken dreams in business than any other. This is because most people are not aware of the distinction between the small business model (primarily retailing products) and the big business model (developing duplication and creating a large team of distributors that produces large group volumes). 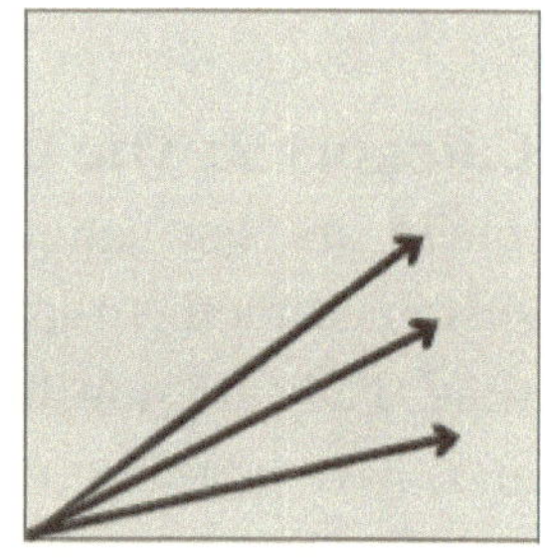

> **Think of network marketing just not as a business, but as a vehicle to help you do the things in life that really matter to you.**

These programs include numerous party plan companies, the phone, and utility services, legal plans, discount cards, air purifiers, new inventions/gadgets, insurance, and other plans that are geared for salespeople. The big problem with these scenarios is that they completely miss the formula for creating wealth in Network Marketing.

Get a large group of people to do a few, simple actions over a consistent period of time.

About 90% of the individuals do not do well in the peddler companies. They may join initially after a good product experience, but soon, they drop out, or remain customers but do not actively build the business.

Category 5: The Holy Grail

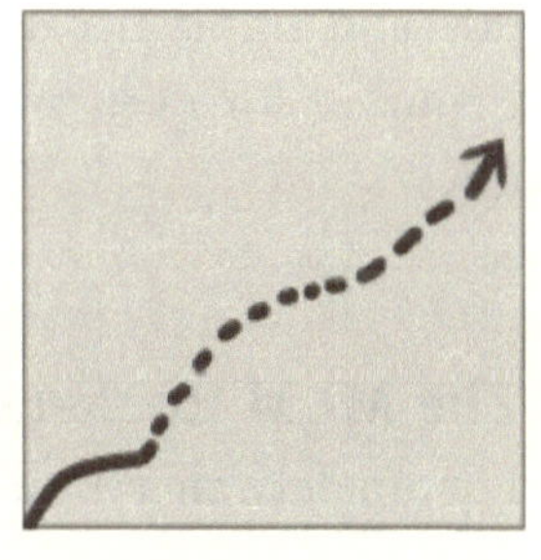

Our final category is where true wealth is created in Network Marketing. These are those emerging companies that possess what it takes to hit and sustain momentum, and become the next billion-dollar success story. This is where legacy incomes and substantial wealth are created.

Every new company believes they are the next "chosen ones". And the distributors who contact you aren't intentionally lying to you. They honestly believe what they're saying. Unfortunately, most do not have enough experience, knowledge, and perspective to really understand what's required for a company to build traction.

> **If you really want to be rich identify a product that all need and no one has... Paul Zane Pilzer**

The MLM Grinders

Because they don't understand the basic principles of MLM, many individuals become "MLM Grinders". These are the people who have to constantly replace their distributors because they drop out. They have to make all the presentations themselves, handle all the meetings, and pretty much do everything. If they slow down for one minute, things start to unravel in their group. They're always grinding, but the recognition, big bonus checks, and free cars and trips always seem a little out of their reach.

Remember the parable about the emperor with no clothes?

Grinders are in a similar situation. They sell lifestyle and talk about residual income, but the sad truth is they don't have either. They work day and night because they're afraid to let up. If they were to stop grinding for even a month or two, their income would shrivel up and die.

The MLM Rockstars

Fortunately, there is a better way. This is the life of the 'MLM

Rockstars', the select group of people in business who are living their dreams. These leaders have rockstar lifestyles with millions in earnings, luxury homes, exotic cars, travel to glamorous locales, and freedom to spend their days however they desire.

Even people who have been in the business for decades often don't realize they are trapped in a grinder cycle with no hope to escape. They keep grinding away, thinking that their big break is around the corner.

What they don't realize is that the situation they're in will never change.

They keep wasting money on ineffective marketing tools, squander effort going to rah-rah meetings, and fritter away the rest of their time trying to resurrect dead distributors.

They talk about duplication all the time, but the only thing duplicating is their credit card debt!

2.1   How to select the right MLM company?

We can examine the prosperous businesses that have developed and maintained momentum in the past and search for similarities among them. Here's a review of them:

1) A sizzle product line

There are many great products in the world, but they aren't all great for Network Marketing. The best products for business are unique, exclusive, and highly consumable.

Some other factors to consider:

The average person has to be able to understand your products in a 30-second elevator speech. If you need 10 lab reports or five-hours long recordings for people to "get" your product, it doesn't meet the formula for creating wealth. This is the reason many flat-line companies do not hit exponential growth.

Are you ready for Network Marketing?

- Are you persistent?
- Are you open-minded?
- Do you really want more out of life?
- Are you willing to put in the time to get it done?

One of the other shocking truths is that one-product companies can't compete in the long run. Like the non-consumables, they can create some initial excitement, but there is not enough volume produced to sustain the compensation plan and reward top leaders. At some point, they recognize that distributors in other businesses with comparable organizational sizes earn significantly more money than they do. So even if they love their product and their company, they ultimately make a business decision and choose to build a business elsewhere.

2) Proper capitalization

This one is pretty simple, yet, it's shocking how many startup ventures don't have enough money to survive the inevitable bumps in the road. This applies to many fly-by-night MLM companies in India as the promoters start the company with little knowledge and even lesser finance. Their objective is to fill their coffers with collections from the company, leaving little to no funds to strengthen the company.

3) Management depth

The managerial and administrative skills of the people on the board is as important as knowledge of MLM.

Unlike any other business, MLM has a unique pulse that can only be comprehended if you have worked in this sector diligently for a considerable amount of time. Companies with normal corporate experience and no MLM experience would not do well as most principles of MLM contradict the traditional business concepts.

4) A Compensation plan that encourages the correct behavior

Since the beginning of the Network Marketing industry in late 1950s, compensation plans have evolved to keep pace with the changing market conditions. Plans that worked great in the 1970s didn't necessarily perform well in the 1980s.

And plans that served well in the 1990s often don't pass the market demands of today.

So, if you are looking for a company to build a strong, solid, and ongoing income, you should look for a company that is offering different ways to earn, most of which should be of the residual variety, and they should pioneer the leveraged bonus.

You have to also see what the plan promotes and support team-building activities, whether the new joiners are paid enough. Most plans reward the agents highly and the individuals at the bottom are paid last and little, demotivating the new joiners, leaving them disillusioned, which causes them to leave.

5) Field leadership

The truth is, no company can give itself momentum. This has to be created by the field leadership—the people who are in the trenches, recruiting, training, and supporting the team.

There are three components that enable this:

- **The System**

  There should be a step-by-step system for you to follow.

  Irrespective of your education level, experience, or age, you'll follow a proven roadmap to building a successful network. The framework provided by the system should stop people from being all about themselves, which is a surefire way to become MLM grinders (networkers who keep working hard but earn little money.

- **Infrastructure**

  An important element of the system is having the proper infrastructure in place to apply it. You'll find powerful recruiting materials such as this social media, magazines, audios, websites, webinar, video conferencing, and many other marketing material in place. Even if you have never been in a company before, you can get started quickly with the help of these resources.

- **Training**

  Another critical element is the training on how you use the system and the infrastructure and we've got that covered! You have the benefit of weekly leadership training calls, webcasts, local, regional, and international training events.

2.2 Beware!

The Federal Trade Commission (FTC) cannot tell you whether a particular multi-level marketing plan is legal nor can it advise you to join such a plan. You must make that decision yourself. However, the FTC suggests that you use common sense, and consider these seven tips when you make your decision:

1. Avoid any plan that includes commissions for recruiting additional distributors. It may be an illegal pyramid. If a plan offers to pay commissions for recruiting new distributors, watch out! Most states outlaw this practice, which is known as Pyramiding. State laws against pyramiding say that a multi-level marketing plan should only pay commissions for retail sales of goods or services, not for recruiting new distributors.

    Why is Pyramiding prohibited? Because plans that pay commissions for recruiting new distributors inevitably collapse when no new distributors can be recruited. And when a plan collapses, most people—except perhaps those at the very top of the pyramid—lose their money.

2. Beware of plans that ask new distributors to purchase expensive inventory. These plans can collapse quickly and also may be thinly-disguised pyramids.

3. Be cautious of plans that claim you will make money through continued growth of your "downline"—the commissions on sales made by new distributors you recruit—rather than through sales of products you make yourself.

4. Beware of shills—decoy references paid by a plan's promoter to describe their fictional success in earning money through the plan.

Before getting seriously involved with any network marketing company a good start would be to check if the company is registered with the government of India. Recently, to safeguard the interest of people at large, the government of India made rules called the 'Consumer Protection (Direct selling) Rules, 2021', and also has started giving out a list of companies registered with the government, this list is refreshed every year.

If you are looking for a company that has been thoroughly scrutinized then a good place to start would be to check if that company has the membership with Indian Direct Selling Association (IDSA) which is an autonomous, self-regulatory body for the direct selling industry in India. The Association acts as an interface between the industry and policy-making bodies of the Government facilitating the cause of Direct Selling Industry in India. To be a member of this organization the company has to go through stringent checks which normally is not possible by any networker, thus it is a safe bet to associate and work with the members of IDSA rather than opting any other network marketing company. Remember, in this industry you not only give your time and energy but also your reputation which is normally tarnished with non-IDSA registered companies.

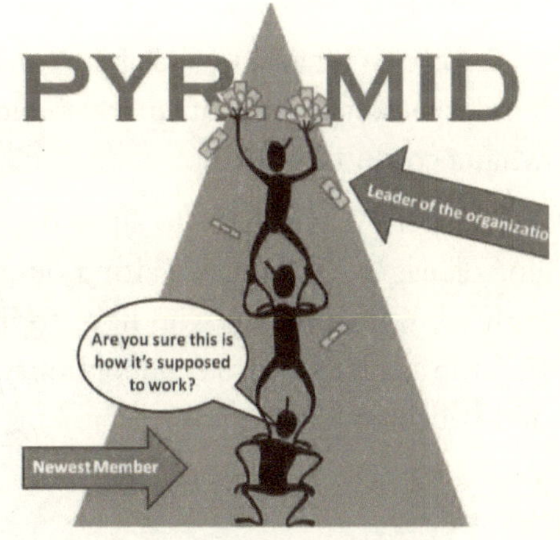

2.3 Miracle Sponsoring

"'Nobody who bought a drill actually wanted a drill, they wanted a hole. Therefore, if you want to sell drills, you should advertise information about making holes NOT information about drills."

Our product is not what you and I, as networkers, really think it is. People don't care about your opportunity. They haven't been waiting all their lives to be an MLM distributor, so why should it surprise you when they say, "No, thanks?" What they do care about, is finding a solution to their problem. Whether that be a lack of money, or time with their family.

Your job is to position your opportunity as the solution to their problem. But you've got some hurdles to jump over in order to do that successfully:

Hurdle 1: You can't sell.

Hurdle 2: People hate to be sold to.

Hurdle 3: Even your friends and family will see you as a salesperson trying to get into their wallets.

People don't want your opportunity. They want the benefits that it can provide them. And they don't like to be sold to but they like to buy.

You want to persuade your prospects that your opportunity is the means by which they can achieve their objectives. The best way to do that is to market and promote information on how to drill a hole, faster, easier, and cheaper.

You don't market your opportunity and products directly. That's what a salesperson does. You market and promote useful information that's what a consultant does.

Experts never have to advertise a sales pitch, yet, they always have a line of eager customers waiting outside their door. It's the greedy, short-sighted, selfish bunch who have to hawk their wares day in and day out. So, stop advertising your opportunity, and start advertising your expertise and your knowledge.

You'll sell more products and sponsor more distributors/agents/associates than you could imagine, with 90% less effort. You will become the hunted instead of the hunter and one of the biggest advantages in doing so is that you don't have to waste any more of your money buying low-quality leads like everyone else.

Reality Check

The first thing we need to do is realize that **Network Marketing is an industry of marketing and promotion, pursued by people who have no idea how to market or promote.**

I know, that's a bit ironic, but it is true. 95% of networkers are employees with no business ownership experience.

This is also why so many upline leaders teach the 'shotgun approach' of making your list of 100 warm market contacts, getting information to them, and seeing who sticks … Anyone can do that. You don't need any marketing skills.

The only reason you're told to make a list and give CDs or your website to 100 people is that your upline knows that you've only got about one or two weeks of emotional enthusiasm about your new business and then the likelihood that you'll ever do anything drops down to about 30% or less.

Pain and Pleasure

Anthony Robbins says that every single action and every decision that we take is based on one single thing:

"The desire to avoid pain or acquire pleasure."

From the length of your hair, to the fact that you opened this email, even the job you chose were all decisions made because they gave you pleasure or helped you avoid pain.

This is crucial for you and me as networkers to know because it will allow us to do our job (which is to market and promote) more effectively.

For example:

> When our prospects say no, it's because the perceived pleasure they would gain from starting a business did not out-weigh the pain of the start-up costs, or moving outside their comfort zone. You can get them over this perceived pain, by encouraging their emotional states.

2.4   Ten Commandments:

1. Everything we buy stems from **emotion**. You bought the clothes you're wearing right now because of how they make you feel. So, if you want to get fewer no's and more yesses when you prospect, you need to realize that buying into a business and a dream is based on emotion. How is buying into this business going to make them feel better? How is it going to help them avoid pain?

2. After communicating the benefits/emotions that can come from your business, you need to help them justify their decision with **logic**, which is what all of us do. You bought into your business because of how it would make you feel if you tripled your income, but you justified the decision to get started with the fact that it's a ground-floor opportunity with an experienced management team.

> **Network marketing is indeed the greatest opportunity in the history of capitalism, and we consider ourselves highly privileged to be able to participate in the industry.**

3. Continually **market yourself** over a period of time.

Everyone's different. Some people will sell themselves within a day or two. Others will take weeks or months. The point we are trying to make is that it has to be on their timetable and not yours, so get rid of the pressure tactics and incentives and you'll start sponsoring higher-quality people.

"We only have a few rules around here, but we really enforce them."

4. Most people are **lazy**. They want better, faster, and cheaper. Any time you can pre-package or manufacture an end result for someone, you're probably going to sell a lot of that product or service. Think about diet pills … You can eat anything you want and still lose weight just by taking our pills.

5. People would rather learn **how** to do something, than actually, do it. They purchase the hope of a result, instead of actually working for it. How many distributors do you have that started their business but never did anything with it?

Distributors fell into the emotional trap we mentioned before and experienced buyer's remorse. They didn't make a solid, committed decision. They gave in to their emotions, and when those emotions wore off, their desire to become entrepreneurs faded away.

Remember,

Nobody who bought a drill actually wanted a drill, they wanted a hole. Therefore, if you want to sell drills, you should advertise and sell information about making holes, not information about drills.

6. Need to make money during your daily prospecting and the key to doing that is to market an inexpensive **retail** product, whether people join your organization or not.

Not only is the money important for financial reasons, but it's vital for your mindset as well. When you have money coming in, even if it's just a few hundred dollars per month, the desperation disappears, the anxiety disappears, checks don't bounce, the spouse stays happy. Their learning curves is paid for, and **NOW**, you have a new retail customer who is easier to bring into the business because a relationship has been established.

7. The real marketers in this industry who treat their business like a **business** do three things:

a. First, they trade generic information.

b. Second, they advertise that information instead of their business.

c. Third, they backend their prospects into their primary opportunity weeks or months down the road after they've already turned them into a paying customer on the front end.

8. The power that comes with social proof through personal recommendations and third-part validation has always played an extremely important role within this industry where we usually find it in the form of **testimonials**.

9. You need to be willing to **give** without wanting before you can have it.

First, understand why other networkers would join you and your business. It's not the product, it's not the compensation plan, and it's not the management team. It's because you are offering a solution to their problem and that solution will only come in two forms:

a. Your knowledge. You, your leadership, and your expertise. They will join you because you can teach them and show them how to build a successful business.

b. You are offering a business building/marketing system that provides a solution to their current problems, and they can see themselves having success using it.

These are the only two reasons a network marketer will ever join you, and these are the two things you must give.

It's not about the opportunity. I have knowledge that can help you become the leader you want to be. So, stop spending yourself broke trying to play the 'mine is better than your game', comparing compensation plan statistics, and sales numbers. Sell yourself. Sell your solution.

Market help—It's not hard.

10. Upgrade your network

a. You need to start thinking long term. We're talking two to seven years down the road. What you do today will have a direct impact on the rest of your career if you have the foresight to plan that far ahead.

This business is 10% about you, and 90% about who you know.

b. You need to professionalize your contact database. This means, you have to start keeping thorough details on each new contact you make. We are not talking about all of your contacts. We are talking about the 'Eagles'—the other leaders you meet, the truly sharp people who already have a track record of success in life and in this industry. Find out who they are, what they are, what hobbies they have, their families, birthdays, etc.

c. You need to find a way to get in front of these people. Now we are not talking about buying genealogy lists and cold-calling to pitch your biz to people. You need to get in front of them so you can shake hands and have a conversation.

d. Next, go to the national MLM training seminars that take place around the country. When you do, you'll notice many of the industry's top income earners in attendance. And guess what, they're not there for the training. Your mission is to build a rolodex of hundreds of other MLM leaders.

We are talking about true networking and relationship building. Your goal is not to sponsor these people today or even next year even though that will happen every once in a while as you meet these people. It's to create long-term relationships and friendships because all it takes is a single leader to change your life forever; and trust me, that is worth waiting for and working for. Professional networkers only work with people they have come to know, like, and trust. It's an inner circle and you have to take the initiative to introduce yourself.

Understand that you (as a stranger), have little to no chance of sponsoring a professional networker. You hold no value to them. Why should they join you, instead of another leader in the company that has something to offer? You have to earn that right. You have to earn that value, and you have to demonstrate it through the relationship that you build over time.

STARTING UP ON THE GREATEST OPPORTUNITY IN THE WORLD!

3.1 Product! Product! Product!

Start by using the products. You must be convinced that they are good and you should have a story to tell. What are the features and benefits, and who are the competitors? By drawing on your experience you will seem convincing and persuasive.

3.2 Know Your Company

Learn as much as you can about the company. Meet the management personally and visit their offices. The more knowledge you have the more effective you will be. Find out the following:

- Who are the owners and what are their track records?

- How long has the company been in business?

- What is the sales volume and how fast is the growth?

- How many distributors are there and how fast is the network growing?

3.3 How Much Am I Paid?

Understand the marketing plan and study it from the company. Ask your upline to explain. Know what bonuses are paid on sales made by you and the downline. Find out what is the effective payout rate. Learn to work out how much money your group is likely to make.

You Are Your Own Boss

You are now the boss of your own business, which means you, can work wherever and as hard or as little as you want since there is no territory. But if you want to do well, you must be prepared to work hard and smart.

"I want to be my own boss, but I'm afraid to
ask myself for a promotion."

Make a To-Do List

The To-do List is the tool that any time management book or a mentor will tell you to adopt. We have one specially designed for network marketers. Make it every day without fail, either in the morning at the start of each day or in the evening of the previous day. We have added a checklist for your daily affirmations (refer to idea number 9.4) and for your daily goal review (refer to idea number 9.8).

Working from Home

You could work from home! John Milton Fogg, the author of *The Greatest Networker in the World*, started his business from the garage of his house. Today's industry with the fastest growth is home-based companies. When I restarted my journey in network marketing in the year 2016, I started by giving presentations in my drawing room or in the prospect's drawing room, until I developed a significantly large team across the country.

Involve Your Spouse in the Business

Make your family a part of your team. A prospect calling your home office and greeted with an abrupt "Hello? He is not home now, call back," does not enhance your image as a professional. Teach your family how to answer your calls. Get them excited about helping you serve your downlines. Praise is the best motivator. Tell others (in front of your family) how good your family members are at answering the phone.

In my entire network marketing career, I never involved my family in the business. I was always a one-man army, but as the team got bigger my work hours and responsibilities increased, plus my spouse was getting agitated as I ended up giving her little time. Only since the last three-four years, I started involving my spouse into the business and today she takes over most of my work, resulting in less work for me, better support for downlines and we spend much more time with each other, especially while traveling as we now travel together.

> **The truth is that we are empowered far less by heredity, luck, and circumstances, then by our vision of what we believe is truly possible for ourselves.**

Teach Your Family to Answer the Phone

- Smile and use a pleasant business greeting.

- Take messages. Never ask someone if they mind calling back later. Trust us, they mind!

- Convey your concern to every customer; "I am sure he would want to speak to you about this. I will ask him to call you as soon as possible."

- Close with: "Thank you very much."

When You Use the Phone Put a Mirror by Your Desk

Sometimes we are not conscious of our emotional condition. By looking at ourselves in the mirror, we will be able to see our mood at that moment and we could smile to ourselves. Strangely, that will change your tone on the phone. If you feel better inside, you will sound better on the phone.

Be Accessible

How easy is it to find you? You might think you're easy to locate all the time. After all, you always know where you are. On many occasions when someone does mention that you are a bit difficult, do you simply dismiss him? Pay attention. I make it easy for them to buy from or join you. Make sure your mobile phone is answered and in case you are in a seminar or a meeting you call back, your email and social media communication should be easily available for your team as well as prospects, whatever it takes be accessible. **If they can't find you they will find someone else.**

Getting Back

Ever left messages and never got a return call? If you are calling long distance, it can be exasperating. Try these ideas:

Message or e-mail ahead to set up a time when you will be calling.

Your Weapon—The Notepad

Keep a small notepad with you all the time. Ideas will come to you anywhere—on the plane or just window-shopping. Jot them down and don't lose them. Many computer programs like Microsoft Outlook come with electronic notes. They are the electronic equivalent of paper stick-on pads. Use these to joy down questions, ideas, reminders, or anything you would write on a notepad.

Success Journey

Keep a journal of your dreams and goals. Keep a record of each day's plans, as well as a weekly, monthly, and yearly plan. You are much more likely to achieve your dreams if you write them down and review them each night before you go to sleep. When you get discouraged, look back over your journal at all you have accomplished.

Your spirits will rise. You will be ready to continue the journey.

Build Your Success on the Success of Others

Network marketing is businesses of helping other people improve their lives. Our business is uniquely structured so our success depends directly on the success we help others create for themselves. If you want to have a little success—help a few people. If you want to have great success help a great number of people.

Passion for the Product

A passion for the product X, supported by a fair marketing plan, is the prerequisite for success in this business, according to Sandy L. Ellsberg, an accomplished network marketer, who says, if you do not love the products, it would not work! Remember, this is about word-of-mouth advertising and unless you can live with the idea of telling your friends about the products which you like or use; don't get involved in this business.

Business Card

The best lesson that I learned from Joe Girard, the greatest car salesman in the world according to the Guinness Book of World Records, is the one giving business cards. Joe says that it is not just whom you know, but who knows you. He related an incident when he went to a football game. There were thousands of people. He just threw a stack of business cards in the air. Someone picked one up, called Joe, and bought a car from him. So be generous when giving out your name cards. It is also important to note how you receive business cards from others.

When they give theirs to you, if possible, ask some questions before putting it away. Remember, a business card is an extension of the person. Handle theirs with great respect. Ask them for a second one to give it to someone who will be interested in them. Then do it.

Being Unique

Make your business card unusual. You have a lot of competition when your business is just one of the many dull, black and white cards in someone's collection. So, think of ways to make your business card different and unique. Wally Amos, the cookie man, attached a tiny sealed package containing a little cookie to his business card. People loved to eat the cookie and keep the card.

> **"If you help enough people get what they want out of life, you will get what you want out of life"**
> **- Zig Ziglar**

Put your picture on the card. Use lots of colors. Why be dull when, with a tiny bit of effort, you can be delightful?

Find the Man with a Dream

Ask people about their dream. The song from the musical South Pacific says, *"If you aren't getting a dream how are you going to make a dream come true?"*

Cecil Rhodes, one of the most successful businessmen of the last century met people who came out to Rhodesia looking for opportunities with the questions.

"What's your Dream?" If they had none, he didn't hire them. Asking people about their dreams shows that you care. It also gives you more avenues to help them and bond with them.

"It's supposed to inspire, but most employees see it as permission to take a nap."

Smile

Smile. Look into the eyes of every person you meet and smile. It makes you look great and feel great. Smiling is the most inexpensive cosmetic on earth.

Office at Home

You can save up to 75% on PCs and recycled office furnishings by buying from second-hand office furnishing companies. Many of your network marketing contacts are excellent office designers, so get free suggestions.

Family

Some time ago, I was sitting at the dinner table with my wife and two children. My daughter was busy telling me about something that had happened in school that day. I didn't hear a word she said, when she had finished, I started talking to my wife about my day without so much as a comment about what my daughter had said. She left the table, and I didn't notice until she started walking away. I then asked her about school. She replied, "I had I already told you, but I knew you didn't hear. Nothing counts but your Network Marketing work." My children needed to know that they were more important than the business.

Balanced Life

Many network marketers show a remarkable capacity for letting their work screw up their personal lives remarkable because solutions are often so simple. At the beginning of each month, prepare a computer-generated calendar of the family and personal appointments for the next 50 days, which incorporates into your network marketing business calendar. This way you can decide what you want to be part of and work your schedule around it.

Family Time

"Don't worry about all the time you spend building your business. It's OK. Your family can do without you for a while," many network marketers rationalize. It's just not true. Families need undivided attention as much as your network marketing business. One habit worth cultivating is to set aside at least one evening a week for a family dinner. Some network marketers bring their children along on business. They could help with simple tasks such as registration, handing out brochures or staffing the booth for a few hours.

Lifestyle

Most network marketers are careful about where their time is going, and the pay-off their network marketing business will have tomorrow. But many people can't say the same thing about their life. Every network marketer should write a "business plan" for their life. Just as we set goals for our business, we must know what we want out of life.

3.4 Why Network Marketing?

Why do you want to be in the Network Marketing business? Many successful network marketers are driven by some experience that they had. It is important to recognize it and share it. It gives you clarity of vision.

3.5 Treat This Business like a Business

Too many people treat this business like a deal or a scheme. They want to go in for a quick buck and then go for another deal. It may make you some money but you might run out of friends pretty soon and you will certainly lose your credibility. The faster you realize that this should be treated seriously like any other business the better the outcome will be.

3.6 Fear

You cannot hide the fact that there will be people out there who, having been exposed to the immense potential of network marketing will still not make it happen for them. They may be totally convinced, go on to read all the material given to them but balk at the first instance of having to talk to someone about it. The big barrier is **fear**—fear of failure, fear of looking bad, fear of being ridiculed; Fear exists when your beliefs are not strong.

The pressure will to offer is not only of value but could change someone's life forever.

3.7 Take Responsibility

Take responsibility instead of blaming someone (the company, your upline, or your downline), making excuses or justifying your mistakes. This business, unlike other traditional businesses, has a number of things that are significantly different. The first is there is a support system inherent in it that is designed to help you e.g., your upline, the company. This is an advantage you will have that most traditional businesses will not have. However, this very same advantage can turn into a disadvantage because people tend to blame others when things don't go well. Distributors have a lot of targets to blame their failure on instead of taking personal responsibility. In almost any other business you have to deal with it yourself.

The second advantage, and also a disadvantage, is that this is a relatively easy business to get into—low capital, using spare time, etc. Once again, when things do not work out well, distributors tend to justify and make excuses instead of learning from it. Because it didn't involve any high capital output, some will simply give it up. In any other business, people will stay and find ways to make it work. Take responsibility from day one and you will win heaps!

> **Those frontline recruits who demand the least attention are usually the ones who become most successful.**

04 PROSPECTING FOR THE BUSINESS

Who Are We Looking for?

There are two different focuses in prospecting for the business. In the first case, your concern is to look for potential customers or consumers. Some of them might join your organization and buy at distributors' price. In the second case, you want to recruit or sponsor new people into your network who would not only be consumers but would also want to be business builders as  well. You will need to look for all kinds and there is no telling what each of them will look like.

To live your dream lifestyle, you got to have many business builders who would help you in selling more products. If you have to move 100 chairs then it's difficult and painstaking for one man to move all 100 chairs, but if you have 100 people then all can move one chair each which would be effortless and with the minimum time taken.

Make the Prospect Feel at Ease

Always create an atmosphere that your customer finds least threatening. Try placing your order/registration form at a visible place while talking to your prospect. In this way, the prospect will be more prepared to sign up when you hand him the form.

Referrals

Ask the referrals for referrals. The whole concept of network marketing is based on referrals from one person to the next. Thank everyone who gives you a referral. Ask them for another. When you call a referral, say, "Ram suggested that I call. I would love to help you find what you need."

Leaving the Door Open

Leave the door open. It may be awkward when someone tells you that they don't want to join your network or use your product. You may feel rejected and get angry. But look for a way to leave the door open. Try to make them feel good, and you will see them again. When the Holiday Inn chain first started its operations, every bank turned down Kemmons Wilson when he asked for start-up loans. He raised money elsewhere and began his business. Then he went back to the original banks and did business with them, too. He could do this because he always "left friends."

4.1   Farming for Pearls

You may be talking to the wrong person. A successful network marketer said that everyone he meets is like an oyster. He will always open them up and see if there is a pearl in them. If there is none, he puts it aside and goes on to the next one. Are you spending too much time with a prospect that has no pearl in him?

Do It-Yourself Advertising

Use everything to tell people about your business. On your envelopes, beneath your letterhead, or in an empty space in your business card or packing of any kind, you can print information about what you are promoting and selling.

> **If you stop building your frontline before you have a solid income, you will fail in this business.**
>
> **No one can succeed by sponsoring only one new distributor every three months.**

Leaving a Trail

Everything you send out should leave a trail for people to get back to you. There are literally thousands of promotional channels that you can use: audio tapes, WhatsApp and SMS messages, brochures, training materials, and handouts—all must have your name and contact on it.

People with No Vision

Q in prospecting for people to join your network, you will come across some who have no vision of what they want in life. Unless you can inspire them and show them what they are capable of, it is unlikely they will be good candidates. They will either not see or will Refuse to see how network marketing can present an opportunity to change their life.

4.2   Keeping Your Calls Short

Try not to beat around the bush or get distracted by other matters when you phone to arrange for a meeting with your prospect. He could be busy, so keep the conversation short. It is also better to explain or talk about things face to face than on the phone.

4.3   Early Bird Catches the Worm

Once you are ready to go with a program, your first task is prospecting for consumers and/or prospective downlines. In recruiting your downline, do this as soon as possible to increase the chances of your contacts joining your network. If you wait, someone else may contact them first and you may find that your "hot" prospects have already signed up under someone else when you call.

4.4   The Prospect List

The first stage of prospecting is developing your contact list. There are no two ways about it. A prospect list is the main tool that you cannot do without. Most networkers I see asking their downlines to come out with 100-200 names each. Most of the new joining will immediately come out with reasons why they can't, but the seasoned networkers would insist that they do it and once they get down to the task of writing it down, it will permanently put them into a different mindset.

4.5   Getting Your First Frontline Distributors

Getting your first frontline distributors is important because these are the people you will be starting off with and eventually devote most of your time to. You may want to recruit a large number of first-level or frontline people to find truly committed people who really work out right. But eventually, you would want to narrow down your focus to only a handful of frontlines distributors, usually a maximum of five to ten at first.

Do not recruit people that you do not get along with.

4.6   Getting Referrals

Referrals are ways to keep your lead list growing. When you have spoken to someone who is not interested, ask for referrals to others that might be interested either in the products or business opportunity or both. Try to get at least three referrals and note any special comments such as the name of the person who has referred you. Getting referrals is important because when you mention a personal reference, the person you talk to would be much more willing to listen. So keep track of who refers you to whom and use these names to open doors when you make your first contact.

4.7 Mining for Diamonds

You will never know who your diamond will be. Achievers in this business come in all shapes and sizes. Some of the people you least expect to fly will soar and on the other hand, those you think will be fantastic may never take off. The best thing for you to do is to offer the opportunity to everyone and give them fair attention. The moment any of them moves, be there to support them as they take off.

4.8 Prospecting Decision Taker

If your prospect is married, invite both the husband and wife together, or if there is someone else in the decision-making process (brother, father, partner, etc.) get them together so that they can see the program at the same time. Then, you won't hear the excuse "I have to talk to my spouse first."

4.9 Prioritize Your List

Once you get your list done, you can prioritize the names (or descriptions) and start working on them, one at a time without leaving anyone out with self-talk like; "Oh! He probably would not be interested? Do not qualify them. Prioritize, yes, but not qualify.

> **Everyone has a definite list of prospects and that list will be exhausted sooner or later. Hence, you must always look for new contacts to give you a fresh list and that way your prospecting list would always be infinite.**

No Name Prospect

Your prospect list does not need to have names only. You can include people whose names you may not know e.g. the girl next door with a cute nose. This business is not designed for supermen or superwomen; just about anybody can do the business. It's an extraordinary business for ordinary people who want extraordinary income. So, anybody can get into your list.

How to prioritize your list:

Prioritize your name list. There are various ways to do that but one set of criteria you can use is;

a)   People who want to improve their financial situation

b)   People who already have a wide network and influence

c)   People-oriented individuals

d)   Experienced network marketers

Prospecting your friend

Your best friend may not be your best prospect! In fact, good friends may end up being the worst demotivator and might try to discourage you. He may do this with utmost sincerity, not having understood the business concept and convinced that you must be caught in some vicious scheme. Work with them like you would work with any other prospect pull, don't push, and avoid trying to convince anybody. Once you have shared the information and opportunity, let them respond to you or otherwise ask them for their concerns. Leave them alone if they tell you that they are not interested. Keep in touch and let them know your successes. Invite them to your recognition events and celebrate your achievements with them. When you get that big check, take them out for a treat and tell them. It might just wake them up to look for you; they know that the door is open.

Prospecting your family member

Similarly, your family member may not necessarily be a priority prospect. They would probably buy your products and be good consumers but whether they will do the business or not very often has little to do with whether they are related to you. The most important thing is not to get upset if our own brother or sister refuses to do business. Do as you do with your friends. Keep them informed and celebrate with them and always, always keep the door open.

Prospect List Worksheet

Some of the people to contact are as follows: Relatives, neighbors, current friends, old friends, school friends, current colleagues, past colleagues, church groups, social groups, interest groups, and people who serve you such as doctors, dentists, hairdressers, etc.

Unless you are talking to people about the business you are really not working the business.

> **Unless you are talking to people about the business you are really not working the business.**

The 'SW' Rule

The cardinal rule in prospecting is the 'SW, SW, SW, SW' rule. The rule is when you go out there to share the opportunity, you come to terms with the realization that "**S**ome **will** do it, **S**ome **won't**." **S**o **w**hat? Because someone else is **w**aiting. This is a mindset that is your ultimate armor against rejections.

Some will,

Some won't,

So, what

Someone's waiting

"There, you see how painless it can be if you just say 'Yes' to joining my downline of distributers."

Cold Prospecting

Work on your Warm List first before you do any cold calling. But always be ready to talk to strangers about your business. Most people you meet will only need a smile from you to get defrosted. Once you have done that (yes, smiley), introduce yourself and ask some questions. What questions? Well, the same questions you want him to ask you like, "What do you do for a living?" As you listen to him, keep an ear out for any hot buttons. Sooner or later, he will ask you similar questions and then unwittingly give you permission to share the business opportunity. The best reply I ever heard a network marketer give was; "I am in the business of helping others make their first million." Would you want to know more, if it was you?

Come up with your own special way of telling others what you do, in a way that they will be restless and eager to know more.

After the Warm List

What do you do after finishing with the warm list? What you need to be sure of is whether you have really exhausted your list. Some would rather go for new markets because they had qualified their warm list and "decided" that they won't do the business. The reason why some people do that is possibly because they still have doubts about the business or the products and would rather work on a less "risky" audience e.g., people they don't know so that if they don't succeed, it would not be so bad on them.

4.10   Inexpensive Publicity

Put up posters or flyers at places you go to such as supermarkets, community centers, restaurants, etc. Carry little packs of literature with you and talk about your business wherever you are. Also, don't underestimate the power of social media. Put posts, reels, update your status with your pitch, and announce to the world your business and activities.

Where to Fish

So where do you find the best prospects after you have really exhausted your warm list? Go back to your criteria for prioritizing prospects (Refer to idea number 4.18) and go to the places where you are likely to find them. For example, people who want to make more money are found in seminars relating to wealth creation or readers of money magazines or success magazines. If you want to be a successful fisherman, you would go to places where the fishes are, wouldn't you?

Testing

Consider all kinds of marketing techniques to get leads as long as you keep focused on the market you want. One example is to advertise, although this could be an expensive exercise. If you have to use advertising, make sure, it works. The only way to find out if it works is to test the advertisement. Come out with a few good pieces and test them to find out which one works best.

Headlines

The headline is important. If you are using marketing pieces to get leads advertisements, social media or letters headlines can make all the difference. Gerry Robert, an international marketing consultant, has an interesting way to find out if your headlines are powerful enough. Just imagine you are putting that headline in the advertisement with a telephone number under it. The question is: will people call? If you feel that people will call on the basis of the headline alone, then it is probably a good one.

Cold Calling

If you are cold calling on the phone to get an appointment, do not try to talk about the product or explain the business on the phone. Focus on getting an appointment. If the prospect is pressuring you to tell him what the business is all about, explain to him that it will take too long, or it is too difficult to do so, on the phone. Keep emphasizing that you only need 50 minutes or an hour of their time to share an opportunity. You do not want to give anybody a chance to turn you down before having a fair chance to share the opportunity.

The key to success; **Believing that what you have is fantastic and having the confidence that whoever you are calling would want it.**

Announcing Your New Downline

One of the best ways to attract the attention of your prospects is to send out information to announce your new downlines. Your prospects may know someone in the list and may wonder why they themselves have not joined the program.

4.11   Give People Reasons Why Others Do It

Buy copies of "Why People join the Network Marketing Business" to give away to your prospects. Also, there are many videos for the same on YouTube. Send your prospects the links for such videos.

Encouraging Visits

If you can convince a prospect to visit the head office or attend the annual conventions, 90% of the time he will be sold on the business.

4.12 Social Media

The latest buzzword in town is social media, which will tempt many of you to wait behind the keyboard to try online recruiting. But logging on to broadcast direct mail messages to online forums or newsgroups can backfire. There are subtle ways to reach prospects through the internet. Go to the business and trade forums of the online services. Now, when a person posts a message requesting  new products or business opportunities, you can answer questions and share the leverage of time to create wealth. At the end of the message, you can suggest a moneymaking machine. Your posting can close with a "business card".

4.13 Hardball Prospecting

Start off by explaining to the prospect that you don't recruit everybody and anybody. You want the very best and the most committed. Ask why they think they should be your distributors. You may lose a lot of candidates but you can be sure that those who signed up with you will last.

> **"New blood is the life hood of any organization."**
> **Continually sponsoring new associates adds vitality to an entire business.**

4.14   Prospect the Man on the Street

Once, a network marketer's car broke down late one night. A taxi driver stopped by and helped him start his car. He was instructed on how to use the time to build riches by the network marketer and ended up recruiting him.

Prospecting the Big Boys

Try checking with the human resource department of larger corporations that are going through a retrenchment exercise. Some have compilations of resumes of employees which they might give away. A good source of information on people to invite to your business opportunity is seminars.

4.15   Tap on Youthful Enthusiasm

If you are not prospecting fresh graduates, you are missing out on a huge opportunity. As a popular Chinese saying goes, "Heroes emerge from youth." Most young people believe that they're at the best age to take the challenge. They have neither spouse nor children to worry about when they're logging an 80-hour week.

Prospecting Everyone

Do you write off physically challenged prospects? Why?

> **"How do you support a large group?" you may ask.**
> **By teaching them three words: "You call me."**
> **And when those calls come, be there for them.**

05 PRESENTING THE BUSINESS AND SPONSORING PROSPECTS

Easy ways to get started

Invite a few friends or neighbors to a presentation at your house. If you feel comfortable, do the presentation yourself. Otherwise, ask your upline to do a few presentations so that you can observe. This will help you get started.

Help them visualize

Help your downline visualize how happy they can be using your product. As a successful car dealer would say, *"Wait a minute. You look so good in this car! Let me show you,"* and hold up a mirror so that they could see themselves as the prosperous, successful, happy owners of a new car! When your downline uses your products, for example, a slimming item, help them see how good-looking and healthy they have become.

Stir their desires

Successful distributors encourage their prospects' desires in many ways. One is by painting such a picture that the person can see, taste, smell, or otherwise experience possessing the product. Or they give the person the impression that they are missing out on a key item or that they would be lost without the object.

"Nowadays, everyone is looking for a second income source," or *"It's the latest thing in town"*—appeals to the desire of not wanting to be left out.

5.1 Benefits, not features

To build interest, stress the product benefits that appeal to the customers' needs. Don't just explain how a product works and why, but describe the benefits these features offer. For example, in promoting a health product, tell the prospect what the product will do for him.

"You'll be able to lose four-five kg within a month, and you'll also get all the nutrients you need because this formula contains all the essential amino acids, vitamins, and minerals that doctors recommend."

Don't start with the functions and constituents of the product like— *"This product has been tested and contains eight amino acids 15 vitamins, and 20 minerals."*

First impression

When you are selling the product, you are selling yourself. The first impression you make starts the process. Continue to back that up. For example, a professional appearance at your initial contact helps to build conviction because you look successful; the prospect imagines that whatever you do must be good if you have been successful at it. You should dress tastefully, have your clothes clean and pressed, get your shoes shined, and handle any sales materials in an adequately professional manner to get that 'success look'.

Likewise, reinforce your image of professional success with an environment that reflects this success, too. For example, pick a meeting place that is nicely furnished that conveys your success. Avoid shady coffee shops, please. And if you are driving to a meeting, make sure your car looks excellent.

5.2 Personalizing the presentation

Avoid a canned sales pitch where people think you are giving them a pre-programmed, pre-rehearsed story, or reading from a script. It sounds phony and is a real turn-off. Instead, speak from the heart and relate how the product has helped you and how it might benefit others.

Sell your prospect on you first. To make people respond positively to your products or business opportunity it is important that they have a good impression of you first.

Use yourself as an example. Making them see how you have benefited or succeeded is a good way of persuading others. One approach is to tell people how the product has changed you.

With how you have got others to join your sales team to market the product, people will notice your success. They will start asking how they can have what you have. What you are, speaks louder than what you say.

5.3   Fishing and not hunting

Another way of increasing your business volume is taking every opportunity to tell your story. Wherever you are, whoever you are with, look for an opportunity to talk about your product or business and how it has helped you. If someone mentions a problem such as being tired, you may offer a solution by asking him to try your product. However, make sure it is an appropriate situation. Don't sound hard selling. Simply share how the product or the company has improved your life.

Drop teasers about your product or business. You can do this in the course of everyday conversation, and then let others ask you for more information. The advantage of this approach is to get people interested and to reach out to you for information rather than have you persuade them to do something. As a result, they would not think that you are trying to sell them something and get defensive. This strategy is particularly good with friends, who might be sensitive to you using your friendship to make them buy something.

Bringing prospects to meetings

You can increase your chances for success when you bring a prospect to a meeting by following these key guidelines:

- If you have set up the appointment several days in advance, call to confirm that you are going to the meeting that day. That way you increase the chances of that person going as previously agreed.

- Pick up the person if you can. This way you make it as convenient as possible for your prospect to attend. Otherwise, they may agree to meet you at the meeting and don't show up. Go to the meeting early, preferably about ten to fifteen minutes before the scheduled time. This gives you a good chance to get a good seat so that you can see everything that is going on and you can also introduce your prospect to others and generate enthusiasm on the benefits to be presented later.

Have your Distributors Agreement and a packet of material readily available to give to your prospect at the end of the meeting. Get your prospect to sign up after the meeting. If your prospect wants to think it over, follow up in a day or two.

Educate

Be an educator. Big businesses are built on educating someone on a concept rather than just selling a product or your company. Educate your prospect on the ideas and concepts behind network marketing such as leveraging time, multiple income sources, etc. A large network is built on recruiting business builders sold on the business concept and not just on consumers sold on products.

Powerful Questioning

Ask compelling questions to pique his curiosity or alter his perspective. Ask him questions that will wake him a little, for example: "If, for some reason, you are not employed tomorrow, do you have another income source that will continue to support your family?"

5.4   Don't push, pull

A person convinced against his will remains unconvinced still. If your prospect is not listening, you are not saying what he wants to hear—stop pushing any more information onto him.

- Always lead with your products and never your opportunity.

- Helping and developing a relationship with others based on their needs and not your own.

- Position yourself as an expert and an authority in the marketplace.

- Use a technique that will enable the prospect to get exposure to your product.

- Have a powerful, attention-grabbing message.

5.5 Ask, not tell

Ask instead of telling. If you spend too much time telling a person, he might end up not agreeing at all. If you ask a lot of questions you make the person think and you stand a better chance of getting him interested.

5.6 Timing is everything

Presenting the business is all about listening to the prospect to understand his needs and then choosing the right things to tell him which will meet those needs. If you find that the prospect is not in a receptive mood and is not really listening, you may not want to talk about the business.

This business has a lot to do with timing. Sometimes, it may be necessary to split a prospecting meeting into two parts because it might not be the time to go into details at the first meeting.

5.7 The four-step sponsoring

The next cardinal rule in sponsoring is: Nobody is going to hear what you are going to say unless you say what they want to hear.

You have four steps to do that:

1. Ask questions and please, **listen!** Ask him what you want him to ask you (Refer to idea no. 4.23 and 5.12) and keep an ear out for his triggers (his needs or what he likes to hear).

2. Build rapport and trust. You do that by finding common ground, from common body language to common interests.

3. Understand his needs. Why do people want to get into network marketing? The reasons range from leveraging time to getting an opportunity to speak in public. Different people have different reasons. Understand them and be receptive to their needs.

4. Present the business in a way that will meet his needs. There are a few ways to do this: Present the philosophy of time freedom or multiplex income, talk about the product, or merely share the money-earning potential.

The shoe that fits

A well-known network marketer has said that network marketing is like buying shoes, you select one and if it does not fit you, get one that does. Nobody in their right mind is going to lose slip over shoes that don't fit. Selecting people is like selecting shoes—it may not always fit and you may have to let some people be what they want to be. We are in the business that might change people's lives but it is not necessarily about changing people.

How Many Do You Need?

How many people do you need to recruit? Kim Klaver, in her audio tape 'So You Want to be a Network Marketer' mentions that the majority of leaders in the industry making US $20,000 or more a month have no more than four legs that produce more than 80% of their income! She also said that the world's greatest network marketer has only 12 legs and now has 25% of the world as his downline. And just one of Jesus' twelve disciples—not all of them—truly betrayed him.

5.8   After joining

Once you have concluded a presentation to a prospect and if you are successful, a few things can happen. He may just decide to try the products in which case you can either sell him some products or get him to join the network and let him buy them at the distributors' price. Let him make the choice.

Henry was a nightmare prospect for network marketing. He couldn't make decisions.

> **You do not need lots of people of your own contacts to be successful in MLM as most of the time you would be working on someone else's list**

If he chooses to join as a customer, sign him up and teach him how to place an order with the company. Get him to call you if he faces any difficulties. If he decides to join the business, you would still want him to get his hands on the products. After learning how to order the products, arrange to teach him how to build the business.

5.9   The first impression lasts

It pays to think about how your downline introduces you to their downline. The way you are introduced can enhance your credibility and therefore encourage their future involvement in your activities including training.

5.10   Tell your story

All network marketers would have their own stories on how they got into the business and what got them motivated to do what they did. The story you tell should inspire our distributors, and as it would be coming from your real-life experience, might also enable some prospects to relate to it. The story could be an ordinary story but as long as it is real, it would be powerful and convincing.

> **We can't avoid crises, but we can prevent them from completely diverting our attention from our work by accepting each one as a stepping-stone to both personal and business excellence.**

DEALING WITH REJECTIONS AND OBJECTIONS

Things Change Every 100 Days

If a prospect says no to you today, it does not mean that he is going to say no forever. It is all about the timing. If he says no to you, tell yourself that now might not be the right time. It is vital that you keep the possibility open and you should never get upset and slam the door shut permanently.

Instead, say something like, *"Thank you for taking the time to explore the business with me. I am still keen to have you join me in this business so I will assume that this is not the best time. Can I count on you to give me a call should you ever want to find out more?"*

Get him to give you a commitment. Meanwhile, give him a call periodically, say, every 100 days. I have seen people's interest in network marketing change from "absolutely no interest" to "hey, remember that business you were telling me about?" in a matter of weeks. The key is to make it easy for him to call you and the possible barrier would be his ego, so it is important to keep that intact.

In the Beginning, Silence is Golden

Absolutely do not let your new distributors go out to make prospecting before they are adequately trained, as not only do they need to anticipate rejection but also be trained on how to handle it. All it takes are a few objections and these will kill your distributor's self-

confidence and beliefs. The worst rejection could actually come from their own spouses! The best thing to do is to actually, forbid him to talk to anybody about the opportunity until you have coached him appropriately.

How to. . .

Meeting objections and rejection is a part of the business. However, if you adopt the 'SW, SW, SW, SW principle' you will go through this unscathed. Out of a hundred persons that you talk to, only about five are going to be your business builders (A's). The rest are either going to be B's, C's, or D's (refer to idea number 7.1). It is, therefore, a game of numbers and there are four important points to remember:

1. Don't treat it like work. Have fun. Tell yourself you have the best opportunity to share with others, and it is unfortunate that some will not get it. And if they don't, just make a new friend. Also, it is a matter of right timing (refer to idea number 6.1).

2. Learn to deal with objections. The best way to deal with that is by increasing your success rate.

3. Increase the number of people you share the opportunity with.

4. Improve your ability to present the opportunity that will fit the person you are talking to.

Somebody once said that if a person really understands what network marketing is all about, there is little reason why he would not want to do it. Unfortunately, most of the time, people are either unable to or do not want to get complete understanding of this industry.

> **Accepting "No" is merely part of the process of finding those who say "YES".**

6.1 Objections Are Good!

Objections give you an opportunity to understand the possible concerns that could be on your prospect's mind. A person who rejects you but won't say anything more than that the opportunity is not for him is a worse predicament. You have no ability to deal with that and the only thing you can do is to continue fishing the objections out of him. Make him comfortable enough to share his concerns with you.

6.2 Objection: I Don't Have Any Money

Possible reply: "Well, that is precisely the reason why you should consider this business. Any other business would require some kind of capital. In network marketing, you need little or literally no capital. To be precise, you only need Rs. XXX to start off. The rest is your desire to succeed and the willingness to put time into it."

6.3 Objection: I Can't Sell or I am Not a Salesperson

Possible reply; "When I was introduced to this business, I had the picture in my mind of me having to go door-to-door selling shampoos. Well, that seems like a picture of the past. We don't sell the way you think selling is. What we do is, we share information on products that we personally use and like."

Or; "I can't sell either. We do have well-crafted training systems, videos, and many training seminars that explain the products and encourage people to buy."

Or; "Let me ask you this—If you see a good movie, do you tell your friends about it? Would you do the same if you came across products that you like? In the same way, we share what we like about our products. This is not selling as such. This is word-of-mouth advertising."

6.4   Objection: I Don't Have Any Time

Possible reply; "I understand how you feel. I thought I wouldn't have any time myself. But I discovered that if it was important enough, we would always find time to do it. Having talked to a lot of people like you, I found that it is important for most people to take time to find a second source of income."

Or; "It is interesting to note that, like you, most people spend a lot of time at their job while wishing to do something of their own. Most of them end up doing nothing about it. So, when I am told that they don't have time, what I believe I hear is that they don't have time simply because they are so busy working for their boss that they end up having no time for themselves."

6.5   Objection: Don't Know Anybody

Possible reply; "Well, that's what some people think. Research states that an average person knows at least 80 persons by name. If you think about it, I am quite sure that you do know at least five persons you can talk to and that would be a good start."

Or: "Would you like to know more people? Well this is a good way to make more friends!"

6.6   Objection: I Will Ask My Wife to Look into This

Possible reply; "I would certainly like to speak to your wife about it. When would be a good time? And by the way, why do you think your wife would be interested?"

Or: "I am glad you want to do that but I also want to let you know that a lot of couples do this business together and they find it fun and fulfilling. So let me share with you a little more."

> **Rejections by the family are by far one of the biggest challenges in network marketing. But you can only change their attitude by changing your own.**

6.7   Objection: I Will Ask My Husband about This

Possible reply; "I am glad you want to do that. I would suggest that I meet your husband with you and share some of the information that you may not be able to answer by yourself. When would be a good time?"

6.8   Objection: Is This a Pyramid?

Possible reply: "I guess you must be referring to pyramid schemes which can generally be identified with two characteristics:

I)   Sale of worthless products or services

II) Requires a large sum of money to be paid up-front to earn anything.

Well, this company I am referring to is legal and does neither."

6.9   Objection: It Is Difficult for Me to Get Other People

Possible reply; "I can understand your concern. When I first joined, I thought I needed to recruit a lot of people and that it would be difficult; Until I learned the power of duplication. Let me ask you this: Would it be difficult for you to get one person a month? If you can do that and if everyone you recruit does the same, how many would you have by the end of the year?" (Refer to idea no. 8.12)

Or: "It would be if you think that this business is about 'getting' other people. However, if you see this as sharing the products that you like and would recommend anyway, or sharing a business opportunity that could help someone earn extra income, then it would not be difficult."

6.10   Objection: I Am Not Interested

Possible reply; "I appreciate your honesty. Although most people would be interested to earn extra income with their available time, I sometimes find that some are not interested because certain aspects of the business may be of concern to them. I would like to learn, what are you particularly concerned about?"

6.11 Objection: Isn't the Market Already Saturated?

Possible reply; "Hardly! The industry is nowhere near saturation. For example, you may think that the market is saturated with retail outlets selling consumer products like shampoo yet there are new retailers opening and new brands of shampoo being introduced every so often."

Or: "Hardly. Tell me, how many friends do you know are actually, actively involved in network marketing as a business?"

"Take two aspirin... recruit two distributers and call me in the morning."

6.12 Objection: I Don't Need to Work Any Harder Than I Do Now

Possible reply; "I guess not and I personally don't think people should. I think we should work smarter and that is why I am talking to you about this business?"

Or: "That is precisely the reason why I went into this business. I learned that it is through network marketing that I can leverage my time to create wealth and not have to work so hard. Let me show you how."

6.13 Objection: I Have Tried It Before and It Did Not Work Out Well for Me

Possible reply: "I am sorry to hear that. Well, I would like to learn from your experience. Can you tell me what went wrong?" (Allow him to tell his story.)

"Thanks for sharing; you have enlightened me on some of the possible concerns that you might have. Let me share with you how this will not happen or is unlikely to happen in this case."

Or; "Can I ask you a question and would you give me a frank reply? If you are an engineer specializing in building bridges, let's say that the first bridge you built collapsed. Would you be saying that it did not work out well for you and therefore you will never build bridges again? Would you not be pondering on what went wrong and make sure you won't repeat these mistakes again?"

6.14 Four Mental Adversaries

Mark Yarnell, a well-known network marketer, has indicated the kind of negatives that you will get when you do prospecting.

He says that out of 200 persons you contact,

- 80 will say no when you ask them to meet up with you (**Rejection**).

- Out of the 120 that say yes, only 70 will turn up (**Deception**).

- Of those who turned up, only 13 will become distributors, 57 will actually not be interested or will just walk out (**Apathy**).

- Of the 13 persons who joined you, only one will stay and eventually make money; the other 12 will leave over time (**Attrition**).

For you to succeed in this business you need to prepare yourself for these **four mental adversaries: Rejection, deception, apathy, and attrition**.

6.15 What You Have in Your Head Will Come True

Some distributors are so fearful of objections and rejections that they will actually end up getting a lot of them! This is because what they carry in their head will "show" through their body language. Your lack of confidence will only end up inviting more doubt on the part of the prospect.

> **As we said in idea number 6.4, objections are good. You must learn to address them and not treat them as if it is going to be the end of the world.**

07 DEVELOPING AND TRAINING FOR SUCCESS

7.1 Categorize your distributor

This is critical to your success in building a large network. Your success is dependent on your success in spending the appropriate amount of time with the different types of distributors you have. Many network marketers get worn out dealing with distributors who appear to have great promise but never truly put their plans into action. You may end up wasting your time waiting for that distributor who never turns up for the meetings for which he said he would come.

'A' Category

These are the people who sign up with the **intention** to do the business and actually get into **action**. They are the most valuable and they are the ones you should spend your time with and pay attention to. You will have to get them on track fast and help them get results as quickly as possible so that they will be continuously motivated.

> When coaching downline distributors, don't make the mistake of telling them what they did wrong. Instead, guide them to do right.

'B' Category

Those that sign up with the **intention** to do the business but never get down to doing it, or have **no action**. These are the biggest time wasters because they are disguised as A's and you would therefore be spending a lot of time trying to get him into action. There are many reasons why he does not get into the thick of the business even though he seems to be initially excited about it. It's quite likely because his belief system is lacking, he continues to have reservations about the products or the idea behind the company, or he simply worries that he won't be taken seriously. It is important that you identify this group and get them into the A's or get them into the C's.

'C' Category

Those who just sign up so that they can buy wholesale belong to this category. They are the consumers and an important group in your organization. Satisfied consumers might eventually become business builders so it is important that you keep in contact and ensure that they are notified of all your business building meetings. They might just walk in one day and surprise you. They require low maintenance. You can increase their value to your organization by regularly providing them with information on products, especially new launches. The goal is to expand their product usage over time.

"D" Category

Those who sign up just to get rid of you. If you are not aware that he actually has no intention of doing the business, you will spend a lot of time chasing after him. Get rid of all your D's.

> **Because of the multi-level structure of our industry, we are all part of a team sometimes coaching and at other times being coached.**

Differentiating A and B

The common question asked is how do you differentiate between an A and a B distributor.

The way to get the B's hiding behind the facade of an A is to reveal them by asking them for a time commitment. You may say something like this, "John, I understand you want to build the business and I would like to commit some of my time to helping you. I would likewise need a firm commitment from you. Would you spend at least 36 hours a month on the business for the next six months?" If he says no he is probably a B and is better off just staying as a consumer until he can make the commitment.

Turning B's into A's

How do you motivate a person who is suffering from inertia and cannot get started, i.e., how do you turn a B into an A? One effective way to do that is to surround him with all you're A's. Introduce him to your active and enthusiastic A's, especially those who have a similar background to his, and let them rub the magic on him.

Nurturing the A's

To ensure that your A's stay as an A you have to nurture him. Constant communication, especially in the first months, is vital. This would be his formative period and it is common that he would be facing a lot of negatives and challenges. You have to be there to lift him up when he is down. Network marketing is a relationship business and the most important relationship that you have is your relationship with your A's

7.2   Practice the reciprocal rule

The concept is that if your distributor takes one step in the correct direction, like giving you his goals, you should recognize him and take at least two more steps with him by allowing him time to go through the goals. This is far more productive than chasing after the B's for their goals.

7.3 80-20 rule

In line with idea number 6.9, practice the 80-20 Rule. Spend 80% of your time with 20% of those distributors that are giving you or will be giving you 80% of your results (or income). This industry is full of NATO's (no action, talk only), Network Marketing has-beens, and Network Marketing academics who are all ready and willing to tell you all their past glories and what could have been and what should have been but are not quite ready and willing to do what matters most work the business and recruit, recruit, recruit.

7.4 Spotting a winner

The biggest regret that most successful network marketers have is spending time on the wrong people. Accept the fact that some people would never do this business no matter what you do, and even if they do sign up and get into it, they will never make much success out of it. Learn when to back off and let nature take its course. We need to know  how to spot a winner. Otherwise, it will be like trying to push a cow up a ladder.

7.5 Learning culture

Build a 'Learning Culture' by constantly asking your downline "What did you learn?" after every learning event. Encourage your different lines to share their learning with each other. Give out articles and recommend books and tapes.

> **As Norman Cousins wrote "the true tragedy in life is not death, but that which dies inside us while we are still living."**

Training: The backbone

Training is the backbone of a successful network. The training of your distributors cannot be left to chance i.e., whatever is readily available from the company. Training must be duplicable with a clear track and the distributor must also be guided individually by the immediate sponsor. Training is not confined to classroom situations which are important events but not to the exclusion of the more powerful one-on-one coaching process. Coaching is not only more effective but also easier to duplicate. Beyond classroom training, it is important to use other tools such as training audio and videotapes, training manuals, and telephone coaching either one-on-one or conference calls, or video conferencing. Once again, the important point is to make it simple and duplicable.

Coaching: The spinal cord

If training is the backbone, then coaching is the spinal cord. Coaching, in its simplest form, is a process of helping a downline learn the business. This could be in the form of debriefing sessions held after a prospecting call—a two-to-one call—or a goal-setting session. While many appreciate the value of this form of on-the-job training, often the opportunity for learning is not maximized. Leaders need to learn to ask the right questions of the distributors in order for them to squeeze every learning point out of an experience. The questions could be:

- What went well and what did you learn from it?

- What did not go as well and could have been done better?

- If we are going to do this all over again, what should we do differently?

- If the person had done so and so, how would you have handled it?

- How would you summarize your key learning points today?

Irrespective of whether or not you go out on calls or oversee a goal-setting session with your downline, a leader should run periodic coaching sessions. Whether you call it a review, a strategic session or a planning meeting, the coaching process will need to be included. This is part of the continuous learning process.

Cultivating a learning culture

Learning is a more extensive form of instruction. Training is perceived as what you do to others whilst learning is what a person does to himself. If you think about it, you cannot make a person learn. In the end, all learning must be self-learning. It is far more fruitful and less time-consuming if you can cultivate a learning culture in your network. You can do so by doing the following;

A. Emphasize the importance of learning new ideas to stay abreast with the changes in the industry.

B. Encourage sharing of ideas and learning experiences among your leaders.

C. Teach your distributors to ask questions. You can do this by asking them for their questions or requiring them to ask you questions after a session, e.g. "As we listen to this sharing session, can we all keep in mind at least two questions that we want to ask later?"

D. Share interesting articles with your downline. You could also give them a list of book recommendations.

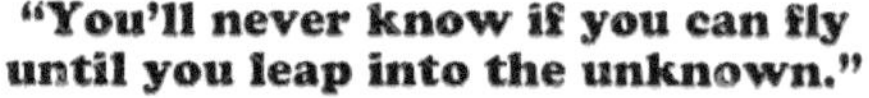

E. Organize reading and sharing sessions i.e., take a network marketing book and assign various teams to read a chapter each, then convene a presentation session whereby each team will present in the following format:

  i) What are the key learning points?

  ii) Which points can be applied and how are you going to apply them?

Audio and video recordings

Another training tool that is powerful and easily duplicable is the mobile phone. These days almost everyone has a smartphone with reasonably good audio and video recording capability. Make it a point to have your training sessions taped so that those who are not there can later benefit from it. The first one that you should consider recording is your standard opportunity presentation. This could serve not only as a training tool but also as a prospecting tool for new downlines.

Focus

You don't have to enroll the whole world. You should focus on working with a few individuals and train them to build a group. Five to ten is a good number. The program works best when you build deep, not wide. The key is to work with a few people and teach them to do What you do.

Training the trainers

Every time you run a training session, make sure you have an outline. Make it available to your downlines and emphasize that they should be able to run the same presentation as soon as possible, assign or nominate people to eventually take over from you.

Areas of training

Training can be divided into three areas: **Attitude, skills, and knowledge.** The amount of training in each area should be well distributed over time. You can divide the training in three phases: Starting up, taking leadership, and going for the stars. The focus required for each phase of training will be different.

> **If you wish to earn a great deal of money and achieve total control of your time and destiny, you must become a leader and conduct your own meetings while teaching your frontline to do the same**

Startup training

Startup training is mostly knowledge-based. New distributors need to get sufficient knowledge about the products as well as how to present the business to their warm market. This phase of training should also provide them with an overview of what to expect in the business and how to deal with initial rejection. At this point, each individual should set his own goals.

Suggested curriculum for a new distributor:

a. One-to-one coaching session with the upline, covering goal-setting and an overview of the product and marketing plan. During this session, he should also go through his prospect list.

b. Business opportunity meetings. He may already have attended one before but he should be there for at least two more for the purpose of repetitive learning as well as bringing his prospects.

c. Product usage training.

d. New distributors' orientation. This should prepare him with the system and the appropriate mental framework to go out to the market and build the business. Techniques on prospecting would be most useful in the initial stage.

Leadership training

This phase of training prepares a downline for leadership as well as provides him with the necessary skills. Besides the periodic coaching and learning sessions, the following areas would be useful:

- To overcome objections

- To conduct a home presentation

- Making a two-to-one prospecting call

- Conducting a product presentation

Go for the stars training

At the highest level of training, you will be turning chickens into eagles. This might involve running a boot camp type of training where you help your leaders to get rid of any 'excess baggage' that they might still be carrying and which will hold them back for the 'final assault at the summit'. Another training session that may be done at this point is train the trainer session.

7.6 Developing people for success

How can you make other people successful? The first thing to do is to be on the success track yourself, after which you can get others to be on it with you and then take the following mentioning process:

- Create a desire in them

- Make them believe that it is possible

- Help them plan a track to run on

- Inspire them all the way

Creating desire

Find out what motivated your downlines to go into the network marketing business. If they are not sure, help them discover the reason, for example, a desire to travel and make friends all over the world. If they know why they are in it reinforce the reason and turn it into a burning desire.

Making them believe that it is possible

Give them all the reasons why they can get whatever they want. Show them examples of people who have made it. Show your sincere personal belief in them and their dreams. For example, if a distributor is in the business as part of his desire is to become a public speaker, give him examples of networkers who became great speakers, and better still, give him video links of great speeches made by networkers.

Helping them plan a track to run on

Provide guidance on realistic timing for step-by-step achievements or milestones. Ask a lot of questions so that they brainstorm and put a plan into place. Remember, this is their plan, not yours, so your role is to help them find the answers, not give them the answers. (Refer to idea number 8.20 on the Lone Ranger Mentality.)

Self-help training

Training need not be expensive. One efficient way to train is through books. Have a list of recommended books for compulsory reading. Everyone in the team must read the books. Also, have scheduled discussions.

Constant motivation

Inspire by setting an example. Motivate them with positive words and actions. Inspire with celebrations and recognition of whoever achieves another successful step towards their dreams.

Product training

Product Training is an essential part of the training curriculum. Like other areas, it should come in manageable doses, varying in length and details depending on the type of products. The first training session should be an overall introduction to the product range followed by basic product usage. The second round of product training should provide your downlines with enough knowledge to share the product with their prospective clients and be able to respond to 80% of their queries. If relevant, the third phase would involve training trainers to run the first two phases.

Learn, do, teach

The simplest format of a self-training process is to learn, do, and teach. Every successful distributor will have to become a teacher. Some people say that network marketing is a training business. Every distributor should get on the learning track as quickly as they can and make it happen in the real world. As they do, they shall then teach others.

Learning to use technology

In this advanced age of technology, network marketing must maximize its immense potential as a business through leveraging technology tools now easily available. Network marketers will be challenged to pick things up quickly, from the internet and email to video conferencing and sophisticated database management.

Communicate with your distributor through email. Help your downlines adjust or invest in computers or even to upgrade theirs. Push yourself and them out of the comfort box into the zone of discomfort. If they felt intimidated by all the gadgets and gizmo, give them a little hand-holding. As for yourself, be a true leader. Take the paths that only a few dare to tread and be at the leading edge of technology.

Sharing training resources

Need more materials? Before you invest in more resources, try asking the top network marketer in your company if you can borrow their curricula. If they do not have what you need, you can at least share and split the cost of purchasing the training resource.

Homemade training videos

Contrary to popular belief, training videos need not be expensive to produce or boring to watch. In fact, for a change, the lower the technology the better, especially if it is produced by the distributors who will be watching them. Try it; it will bring a lot of fun and laughter.

Training Test

Before any training session, tell your distributors that you will be giving them a test. It is the only way to force them to learn the material. Giving them a test will also help them to internalize the training.

08 HOW TO DUPLICATE AND BUILD A LARGE NETWORK

Lead by example

We hear a lot about leading by example in the corporate world. In network marketing, it is the rule. Distributors are an empowered lot and will not simply do what they are told. They only do what they see their leaders do and only if it works. As a leader, I can't not get my team to stand in the middle of a busy shopping mall handing out invitations to an opportunity meeting unless I start doing it myself. In this business there is only one way to lead—in the front and facing the bullets.

Getting help

Running a network marketing business requires certain management skills. If necessary, you may have to hire someone full-time to assist you with the business. When Mark Victor Hansen was on a speaking circuit, he brought along his manager to expand his network marketing business. If your network grows to a huge size, it may be worthwhile to consider engaging an assistant to help you build the business.

Masterminding (core team)

Form a group of masterminds consisting of the key, active leaders in your network. The main objective of the mastermind is to find ways to help each other grow the business and to support each other's goals and aspirations. The concept of masterminding came from Napoleon Hill's book *Think and Grow Rich*. In mastermind meetings, the agenda could cover the following: What are their plans for the coming week? What are the concerns they face? What can we do to help each other?

Principles of Masterminding

Gerry Robert in his program 'The Money Master Boot Camp' laid down the following principles for masterminding:

- Be committed to the mastermind group

- Be committed to giving rather than receiving

- Help without looking for anything in return

- Speak in positive terms and engage in no limit thinking

- Respect your partners and agree to build your relationship and business on trust

- Support the aspirations and goals of your mastermind partners

> **If you wish to earn a great deal of money and achieve total control of your time and destiny, you must become a leader and conduct your own meeting while teaching your frontline to do the same.**

- Become accountable to your partners. Do what you have agreed to do. Take action

- Be honest, positive, enthusiastic, expectant, and ready to contribute 100% to your group

8.1 Sponsorship

In the course of building your network, you might come across a distributor that you have recruited, who has indicated good potential but couldn't give full-time commitment due to financial constraints. You may want to help him go full-time by providing him with financial sponsorship to support him until his bonus cheque is big enough to take care of his needs. If you have to do this, keep two rules in mind:

a) Make sure that the arrangement is performance linked. For example, the financial sponsorship continues only if does not stop seeing at least two new prospects a day.

b) Make sure that the arrangement has a timeline to it. It cannot be without an end.

If you want to embark on this type of scheme, monitoring is the key.

8.2 Profit sharing

One network marketer faced two big challenges when he tried to expand his business: stretching more of his time and creating equal opportunities for his downlines. He nailed both with one solution: Asking his key distributor to invest in a training center, in return for a share of the profits it generates from recruitment and product sales. His downlines now have a place they could call their own and became more motivated in the business.

Preparing for your trip

What you get out of a business trip depends on what you are looking for. If you do not want to miss your goal, you have to be willing to not get distracted by things that aren't on your agenda. To make the most of trips away from home, you must keep lists of the people you know by city of residence so that you could visit them when you are there.

Meeting agendas

Your distributors may resent attending meetings with an open agenda or no agenda. The best meetings have a clear focus, a distinct purpose, and a time limit. They also have agendas that are circulated in advance to everyone attending, so that they can prepare their thoughts beforehand.

Business volume

Put your emphasis in the right place—on business volume. Whether you are selling to the ultimate consumers or building a network, always emphasize on business volume. This statement may be common knowledge but many people lose sight of these principles and only seek to recruit distributors, so they focus exclusively on building a large group. The only way you can make money in network marketing consistently is by keeping a consistent business volume because bonuses are only paid through that. Once the focus on moving the products is properly emphasized, create a network and look for key distributors who would likewise focus on marketing and promoting the products while building a network. The reason for the emphasis on the product is that whether you personally sell the products or have a network working with you, you and or your group must move the products, otherwise, you won't make money.

> **You can have any income you desire by becoming a positive influence in the financial destiny of others. So be good to your distributors and they would be good to you.**

8.3   Independent distributor

Teach your downline to never ask the upline to do what they can do by themselves. Help them, certainly, but do not handicap them. This can start off from day one e.g., by filling up the registration form for your downline. Never fill it up for them, let them do it themselves and if they have difficulty, only then offer your assistance. This may seem petty but it will set a bad habit if you do otherwise. Imagine what might happen if you are not there and he has to sign up his own downline and he doesn't know how. What will he do? Call you? If they can't do something in the beginning, make sure they learn. Coach them well by doing it with them e.g., talking to a prospect, and make sure that they realize that they will eventually not only have to do it themselves but also teach someone else later.

8.4   Quantity or quality?

The key to building a huge return on your network is building a huge network, which has a huge business volume. Big bonuses come from big business volume (BV). But there are two issues here:

- **Quantity** i.e. lots of downlines in your organization, and

- **Quality** i.e. lots of active downlines with consistently good business volumes.

I was once asked: "So, what do we focus on? Quantity, which is getting as many people into the business as possible, or quality, which is getting good producers into your network?"

My reply is to have both, but the real focus is neither. The focus is **Quality Duplication**.

The power of duplication

Build quantity into your network. If you are in the network marketing business and you have not fully comprehended the power of duplication or the principle of multiplication, you have obviously missed out the entire essence of the business.

Even for those who understood it, the common failure was not being able to use it. To convey the concept, I often ask, "If you recruit only one person a month and if every person you recruit does exactly as you do, how many persons you would have in your organization by the end of the year?" I then remain silent and let my listeners squirm while finding the answer. When I finally tell them that the figure is 4,096, you can see the widening of their eyes and mouths as the principle dawns on them.

Then they ask, "How do we do that?" The answer is Quality Duplication.

You can build a network of 4,096 downlines by recruiting one person a month for 12 months, provided you have 100% perfect duplication. The reason why most people couldn't do this is that they could not get 100% duplication (if any!) How large a group you can get, therefore, depends on how well it is duplicated.

The system must rule

Quality Duplication is the key to building a huge and profitable network. To ensure duplication you need a system i.e., processes that anybody and everybody can follow and teach. You cannot duplicate a person but you can duplicate a system. Ray Kroc, the founder of McDonald's cannot be duplicated but the McDonald's franchise system can be and is, to almost 100% perfection in 18,000 outlets worldwide. In building a successful and long-term network, the system must rule.

8.5 No perfect system

To make sure you duplicate well, follow the system you are provided with religiously.

- Do not try to "do your own thing" until you have built up a large enough network of your own and you have good reasons to make any changes.

- Even if you have, don't until you have discussed it with your successful and active upline and leaders.

- Even if you have done that, don't; unless you absolutely, definitely, irrevocably cannot use whatever you have got.

There is no perfect system and time is better spent perfecting your ability to duplicate the system rather than perfecting it.

Building a system

When you have to come up with a system on your own, remember, a system is only as good as it is duplicated. A system is a collection of processes e.g., a process for recruiting someone or a process for going through the first month of learning.

It is of paramount importance that it is clear, simple, and written down. To ensure quality duplication, you will have to do the following:

- Involve your leaders in formulating the system: "We commit to what we ourselves create."

- Emphasize the system at every opportunity, preach it, and follow it.

- Ask your own leaders if what they are doing is duplicable. That way you keep them focused 80% of the time on duplicable activities which translates into the system.

- Get your leaders to review the system periodically in the initial stages. That way you can monitor the possible deviations and adopt possible improvements.

- The way to test whether the system has taken root is to ask yourself if downlines' activities will continue (as they should) when you go on a long holiday. Will McDonald's still be around after Ray Kroc's has gone away?

Borrow a system

If you are not given a system to run the business, ask for one. If you cannot get one from your uplines) borrow it from a successful sideline. It would be foolish to use a system from an unsuccessful distributor. Be cautious about using anything which has not been tested on your company. What works for XYZ Company may not work for yours, even if the principles might be similar.

Reinventing the wheel

How do you prevent your new distributors from reinventing the wheel? You should do the following:

- Insist that they follow the system and not deviate for at least the first few months, say for six months. If they do deviate, you should be consulted.

- Give them reasons for doing what they should be doing and tell them about the consequences of not duplicating.

- Make system training mandatory

- Anticipate the deviations early and advocate that they stick with one system long enough to enable results to show.

- Anticipate that they will be exposed to other leaders, who may be singing a different tune, and prepare them to learn new ideas without necessarily changing to another system.

"Ralph is doing a preliminary study of re-inventing the wheel."

> **As many as 95% of those people who remain in this industry for a couple of years or longer reach the highest levels in their respective companies. Whatever you do, just don't quit!**

Tools

Design tools around the system that you have adopted if they are not already available e.g., time management tools, checklists of questions to ask a prospect, a worksheet to record your prospects and action taken, standard letters, a goal-setting form, a training tracking sheet, criteria checklist for evaluating a network marketing company, a presentation flip chart, training recorders, and pendrives. These tools help to make the system work for your distributors; once again the key is simplicity.

The D-Question

To ensure you do things that your distributor can learn from and duplicate, use the D-question. Here 'D' stands for 'duplicable'. Ask—Is what I am doing duplicable? From the meetings to the prospecting techniques, you use: "Is it simple enough to be duplicated?" Keep asking yourself the D-question and if you answer 'yes' at least 75% of the time, you are on track.

The Lone-Ranger Mentality

Almost all youths are brought up to worship a hero of some sort, from the Tarzans of previous generations to Rock and Rambo today. It is good to be a hero. Heroes swoop down in times of trouble and get rid of the problems i.e. the bad guys. We learn from the young that such behavior will be cherished and held in high regard. So, deep down, we all want to be heroes.

Mine was the Lone Ranger. I switched on the TV and the story would start showing a small town in the West, with a lot of trouble because a gang of bandits have come into town and kill the Sheriff, abuse the pretty ladies and terrorize the town folk. They are helpless. There is nothing they could do to solve the problem. Suddenly, from a distance, a man in a mask comes riding a horse in full fury. He is none other than the Lone Ranger. Needless to say, he shoots the bad guys, kills a few of them, and chases the rest out of town. The whole town rejoices and all the folks come out to worship him. He has solved their problems for them. But Lone Ranger has to go, so he rides off into the horizon.

Next week I switch on the TV and what is the story? Similar town, similar problems, week after week. Network marketers are the same. A lot of them want to be heroes, riding from town to town solving distributor's problems for them when they should be teaching them how to solve their own problems. In this case, don't try being a hero. It feels good but it is tiring. You can duplicate a system and a set of processes but you cannot duplicate a personality.

8.6 Leverage

The best tool to turbocharge your journey to success is leverage. Leveraging means getting more done with less. In this business, you should constantly look for ways to leverage other people's time, experience, expertise, and energy. Then allow others to do the same on yours.

Franchising and Network Marketing

There is a common fundamental shared by the two most exciting and fastest growing business methodologies: franchising and network marketing. The fundamental is that both exercise the power of duplication. Whilst franchising has gone through its initial years and has since established its credibility in the business world, network marketing is still working hard at earning its due respect although at an increasingly rapid pace. As network marketers, it will do us good to learn how to 'franchise the business' in order to help us build a large network.

Franchising the business: Emphasize duplicability

Franchising a business concept excels in its emphasis on duplicability. In fact, the franchisee buys and pays for the duplication. Its adherence to a model of success is ingrained in the business from the beginning and often enforced by the franchisor. In network marketing, this element is not given enough emphasis, and in some cases, not even required and is seldom enforced.

To do: Emphasis on duplication in the early stage of the business is crucial. One way is to give all new distributors an example of the power of duplication (Refer to idea number 8.12).

Franchising the business: The operations manual

One of the key elements that will contribute to the success of a franchise is the operations manual. In many cases, this becomes the Bible' for the franchisee to use as a guide to the business. In network marketing, guidance on how to run the business is often verbal and seldom consistent, depending on which upline you talk to.

To do: Leaders should develop a simple 'operations manual' that can guide the system on how the business should best be conducted.

Franchising the business: Selecting the franchisee

In franchising, you never really **sell** a franchise but you **select** your franchisee. You make sure he meets certain criteria before you "award" him the franchise. In some cases, they have to go through a series of training. In network marketing, networkers "sell" people into the business and this goes for anybody who wants to build the business. No criterion is required and all you need to do is to sign the application form and buy the products. We are not suggesting that you now go and "select" your distributors. But there are certain powerful elements that we can copy.

To do: Make all new distributors who want to build the business undergo a trailing lasting at least a month. and completion of a series of assignments e.g., to try all the products, make their name list, attend four meetings, etc. before he "qualifies" and gets "selected" to go into the next stage of development where he gets more attention and more details of the System. For those who did not, give them more time or let them do it their way.

> **Distributors, who have stayed with one company for many years, and built new legs in each of these years, are now very wealthy.**

Don't quit

To be successful, you must persist. Your business may seem to grow slowly at first. Don't make the costly mistake of throwing in the towel. It will take a bit of time before everything will fall into place, and your group will begin to grow at a faster and faster pace. The one thing that's true for every single successful network marketer in the entire world is this he or she didn't quit.

To be an eagle, mix with eagles

Associate with successful people. There is a saying, "If you want to be an eagle, mix with eagles and not, chickens." Stick around people who made it. Talk to them and ask them how they do it. Learn from them. Observe how they dress and talk. You will notice that they are positive, enthusiastic, upbeat, humorous and fun.

Techniques to keep you motivated

Set a goal for yourself and when you achieve it, give yourself a reward. Put up a picture or photograph of something that you want, such as a holiday, car, or house. Look at them daily and visualize you getting or enjoying them. These will be a constant reminder to get you going. Compete with yourself. Don't worry about what others are doing. Realize your own potential and focus on achieving your own goal. Read about the success of others. Read biographies of successful men and women. Identify with their experience and inspiration. Motivate yourself by motivating others. The more you teach, the more you learn. So, find ways to motivate others, you will find that the effort will motivate you too.

9.1   Example of Affirmations

- I draw success, abundance, and good things to me.

- I surround myself with wonderful, beautiful, successful people.

- I have perfect abundance in my life.

- I have everything I want or need.

- I am living the full life I want.

- I have a wonderful family, a beautiful home, the car I have always wanted, and I can travel whenever and wherever I want.

- I have a winning, persuasive personality, and when I eagerly tell people about my business, they are eager to participate, too.

- I am strong, powerful, and have absolute control over my life.

- I have attained my goal of making Rs. 5 lakhs a month in running my own business.

"When you've finished your affirmations, dear,
don't forget to put your trousers on."

Things to do to feel positive

Place encouraging signs all over your home, then take a tour around it to look at them. For example, you might make up some posters that say:

- Winners never quit. And quitters never win.

- When you're down you're not out; unless you think you are.

- There are no failures, just temporary defeats.

Review your affirmations or goals. Visualize yourself attaining them now or take a break from whatever you are doing and do something you usually like to do (for example, playing golf, going to movies, dancing).

> If you visualize the new, you gradually begin to shed the old, believing with every fiber of your being that what you visualize is happening to you at that very moment. This is when change begins to occur.

Think and grow rich

Have a clear picture of where you are going and what you need to do to get there. Napoleon Hill suggested the following in his book:

- Form a specific, clear picture of what you want.

- Determine what you need to get there.

- Develop a plan of action.

- Obtain the tools, techniques, or personnel you need to put that plan in action.

- Set a date for achieving it.

- Begin at once.

Making it achievable

Create your action plan to achieve your goals. Turn your targeted number of product volume and number of people you want to recruit into smaller, manageable chunks you can work with on a daily, weekly, and monthly basis.

9.2 Review your goals

Review your overall goals regularly. Consider the following question;

- What are my current goals?

- What are my most important goals?

- Do I want to change any goals?

- What is my timeline for achieving these goals?

- What do I need to do at each of these periods to go where I want to go?

9.3 Start each day with a prayer

Thank you, Lord, for my customers and my friends. May you bless them abundantly and may all their fondest dreams come true.

We are all dependent on our friends and customers. We are happy about their success. If they are successful, we can be successful too.

> **Either you deserve a life of financial security and family time, or you deserve to live a mediocre life amidst negative people. It's up to you.**

Under-promise and over-deliver.

Do what you say you will do. Don't let people worry. Call them, send an email, write or fax. Let them know you care enough not to let them down. If something unforeseen really happened, communicate with them, don't let people wonder. Be reliable. Be on time. Build a reputation that can be counted on. It is the wisest thing to do.

Praise and reward

Praise and reward your downline. Put a little love, care, and attention into the business. Find unusual ways to congratulate people. We took a group of downlines who had achieved certain results on a short boat cruise and played a game called the 'Manitou Game' to teach them how to praise and reward. Everybody was assigned a *Manitou* (a loved one) without knowing who the person was. Throughout the cruise, the manitou had to shower love, care, and attention on the person without revealing his identity. The last day ended with a 'Guess who your *Manitou* is' and an exchange of gifts. Everyone had fun, felt great, and was rewarded.

Be interested

Establish eye contact with your downlines. Actively listening to someone and making notes as someone talks is irresistible. In conversations, try being interested, rather than interesting.

Hopes and dreams

To reach your goals, draw out other people's hopes and dreams. Reverend Bob Richards, an Olympic gold medalist in pole vaulting and a national decathlon champion who often speaks to high school students on motivation, told us he would often conclude a presentation by saying: "There is an Olympic champion right here in this auditorium! One of you is willing to pay the price. You know who you are. Thank you." After many such speeches, some least likely to succeed—fat, short, skinny, or underdeveloped—children would come up and say to him, "Mr. Richards, I'm going to be an Olympic champion!" or, "I'm going to win a gold medal in four years. I'm the one!" And many of those unlikely kids were 'the ones!' They believed they could do it. They answered the call and went on to become Olympic champions. Draw out the dreams, goals, and hopes of all you meet. One network marketer we know introduces some of his downlines as "diamonds-to-be".

Plan to win

Have you ever noticed that some folks may achieve a small success, and then seem to do everything they can to stand in their own way? They don't have a plan to continue to win. Spanish conquistador Hernando Cortes conquered all of Mexico with a handful of men, a few horses and a plan! The Spanish ships landed at a port called Vera Cruz. Cortes put his plan into action. By gathering warriors from the local tribes who were tired of being tyrannized by Montezuma and his armies, Cortes organized a huge army of natives, led by his men. Then he made a master plan to march against Montezuma. However, the Spanish soldiers were afraid. They went to Cortes and said, "Boss, your Plan A to march against Montezuma and win is great. But let's put together Plan B. A safe plan of retreat back to our ships."

Cortes replied that he would think it over and get back to them the next morning. At night, Cortes sent out his personal servants to sink his own ships in the harbor! At dawn his men were thunderstruck. "What about Plan B to retreat to the ships?" they cried. Cortes answered, "We are going with plan A. The plan to win!"

Do it for others

Be proud of your work. An 80-year-old multimillionaire was asked, why he was still working so hard? The millionaire replied that he doesn't need the money, but there were others working for him who do. He was proud to create opportunities for others.

Love your work

Love your business, industry, or profession. If you are in a field you don't like, don't hang like a dead weight around your boss's neck. Who wants to do business with, or promote a miserable complainer? Get out and find something in which you can be swept away. Love your work so much that when they ask you how many hours a day you work, your answer is not; "As few as possible," but, "As many as I can! I only wish there were more!"

Confucius said, "You will never labor a day in your life when you find work that you love passionately."

9.4   Picture it done

Put up a picture, a figure, and words that form the goal you intend to reach. Put it where you will see it every day. Conrad Hilton used this method for achievement. He always put up a picture of each hotel he dreamed of buying. Then he made the dream come true.

Do call me, I can't call you

Teach your downlines to call you instead of having them expect you to call them. This would save a lot of time and would make your work a lot easier. To ensure this happens, keep encouraging them to call you or send an email to you. If they do, and you are not immediately available, make sure you return their call or email them back.

Set them free

If your downlines don't call you and don't seem to need your help as much, don't do what most dotting mothers do to their grownup kids—feel a sense of loss and end up nagging them or overprotecting them. Your downline will always be there and you, likewise, you should always be there for them whenever they need your help. Give them a call occasionally to see how they are doing but let them be.

9.5   Recognition

Recognition is vital to the continued health of your network. This ranges from words of appreciation you can say to your downlines for little things they do, to full-blown dramatized affairs like sending, a limousine to chauffeur your high achievers around for a week. People quit the corporate world because they are not recognized for their contributions. Let your network be full of it. And don't just rely on company-organized recognition, do it yourself as a leader.

Negative up, positive down

Teach your downlines to keep any negatives away from their downlines and tell you about them instead. The rule is 'Negative up, positive down'. This is important to keep your network positive, alive, and growing. Be responsive to their negatives and do not be defensive. You may not always be able to do something about it. Nevertheless, you should try and that is what matters more to your downline.

You got to have fun

Make the business fun. If you and your people don't enjoy it they won't do the business for very long. Reduce the drama and the stress, and focus on sharing and caring. This is what network marketing is about.

Let your enthusiasm show

The most important belief for you to cultivate is the belief in the possibilities of network marketing, your company, product, and opportunity, and most important of all, your belief in the possibility of success for yourself and all the people you talk to. When you're discussing your program with others, make sure you let your enthusiasm show. Remember, what you say isn't nearly as important as how you say it.

Do the right thing, not just do things right

Do the right thing and not just do things right. Don't confuse activity with productivity. There are three things that will build your network marketing business:

- Developing consumer base

- Sponsoring distributors and

- Helping your people duplicate your efforts.

9.6 50 reasons for failure

1. No written goals. Doesn't know what he wants out of life.

2. No directions, visions, or dreams. **Confused** and lost.

3. No serious **commitment** to the business. Hence, no serious action is taken.

4. **Gives up** too soon. Usually quits in the first 90 days.

5. **Lazy**. Wants to reap the rewards of his downlines' efforts without working.

6. Doesn't establish a **retail base** in his business.

7. Doesn't **work** his business on a daily basis.

8. **Resentful** of upline's earnings. Stops producing to prevent his upline from receiving bonuses on his production. This is a self-defeating attitude.

9. Constantly **blames** and finds faults with the company, the products, the marketing plan, lack of support from his upline, etc. Doesn't realize that if others can succeed under similar circumstances, he can too.

10. **Unrealistic expectations** for the little effort that he puts in.

11. **Impatient.** Wants to make big money too soon without being willing to put in the necessary effort.

12. **Complains** too much and acts like an immature crybaby. A non-producer.

13. **Easily influenced** by negative comments from family members, relatives, and friends. Doesn't listen to the positive side. Can't think for himself.

14. Always gives too many **excuses**.

15. Thinks he **knows** everything.

16. Keeps **switching** to other network marketing companies without first achieving some degree of success. Never makes big money.

17. Wants to sponsor **top producers** instead of learning how to become one himself. (It is better to be sponsored by a Top Producer than to sponsor one. That way you can learn HOW a Top Producer achieves. Mentioning that your sponsor is a Top Producer is a great recruiting tool.)

18. **Disorganized**. Wastes too much time looking for documents. Cluttered desks.

19. Poor **record keeping**. Doesn't keep accurate records of transactions.

20. Only interested in **personal profit**. Doesn't care much about the needs of his customers and downlines.

21. **Uninformed** on how to succeed in network marketing. And not interested to take the initiative to find out.

22. Can't be **reached** easily by customers or downlines.

23. Doesn't **return calls** promptly.

24. Fails to keep **agreements and appointments**. And then doesn't explain why.

25. Doesn't **follow up** on prospects and customers. Doesn't show that he cares.

26. Gets **discouraged** by small problems and inconveniences. Hence, slows down effort.

27. **Bad mouths** other companies. Loses credibility as a positive person.

28. Is not **serious** about network marketing.

29. Lacks **self-esteem**. Drives around in a messy, dirty, and unpolished car. Doesn't realize that prospects see this as a person who has a poor self-image.

30. Distributes **unprofessional**, sloppy, poor copies of information.

31. A poor **example** of the benefits of the products that he represents.

32. Doesn't really believe in the **products**.

33. Doesn't handle customers' or down lines' **complaints.**

34. Doesn't **recognize or praise** downlines' achievements or performance. Too self-centered.

35. Hangs around **negative** people instead of top earners. Birds of a feather flock together. Beware!

36. Doesn't pass time-sensitive **information** to downlines immediately.

37. Spends too much **time** getting organized and too little time talking to prospects and customers. Hence, he has the tendency to avoid people.

38. Expects **perfection** from a new company without realizing it takes time.

39. Doesn't take time to **plan** for success in his business.

40. Has an unprofessional **appearance**.

41. Doesn't **read** nor is updated about the latest happenings in the industry.

42. Physically **unfit** so lacks the energy to put in the necessary effort to succeed in the business.

43. Doesn't strive to do his **best**.

44. Believes in rumors. Doesn't check the facts. **Gullible** about any program.

45. In the **wrong** network marketing program.

46. Doesn't believe that: **"If it's to be, it's up to me!"**

47. Gets involved in **chain letters**, illegal pyramids, and other schemes.

48. Depends on **spill-overs** of other people's efforts.

49. Unwilling to **take risks** such as investing in advertising, brochures, flyers, etc. Too security-conscious. He waits and watches things happen instead of making things happen.

50. Takes a **"no"** personally ("No" only means "not right now. Give me a good reason to say "yes.") Hence, he stops making efforts to call people.

9.7 Low-cost advertising

In marketing, you have to spend money to make money. However, the rise of social media and digital marketing has made it easier and quite inexpensive to market a business. They can reach targeted customers with effective and low-cost marketing ideas for networkers.

Below are some of the ideas

A) Create a **Google My Business account** for free, this free account can make your business show up in Google searches and people can easily find you. You will also get your business on Google Maps, which is a huge plus. Moreover, it will help you to reach out without spending a penny.

B) Content marketing is one of the least expensive creative marketing strategies that allows companies to create fresh, interesting content, publish, and distribute content for a targeted audience on the internet. Online lead generation is key to acquiring new customers. It does not require a large investment and can have a significant impact on your bottom line. There are many approaches you can use, such as you should set up a blog to keep your readers informed and entertained. This is done by adding new and interesting content every now and then so they never get bored

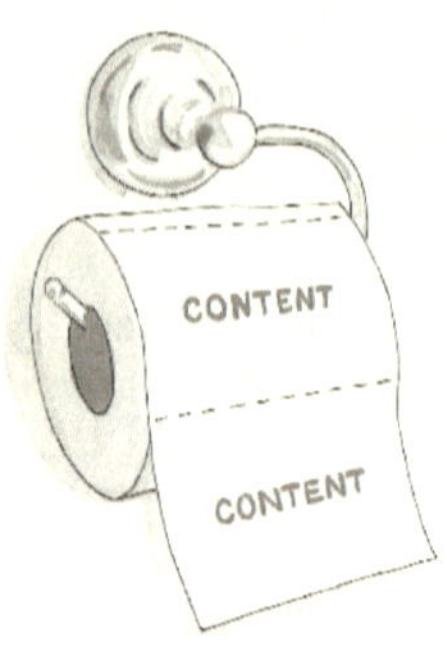

C) Infographics, videos, podcasts, ads in newspapers, and promotional posters are just a few startup marketing ideas that can pertain to content marketing. They're especially good at catching people's attention.

D) Post (and engage) on social media: You can use channels like social media and blogs to grow your business for free and enhance your brand with personality. This will help you develop trust with a new community online. Create business accounts and participate in the big social media sites—Facebook, Instagram, LinkedIn, Twitter, YouTube, and more. Having a few spare minutes? You can do one of the following:

- Use social media sites to promote your latest blog posts. This will help you to drive traffic, as well as increase the number of followers you have.

- Directly speak with followers to express your brand voice and encourage engagement.

- Run polls on How can we improve on ideas?

- Take excerpts from longer forms of content and create quick and informational posts that are easier to digest.

- Whatever your reason, if you want to make the most out of social media in your business, be sure to maintain a regular presence and take initiative on the social media platforms you set up. Ensure consistency, community, collaboration, and commitment.

E) **YouTube**: Now that we are exploring our way through e-commerce, let's discuss this appealing option as well i.e. YouTube, the second-largest search engine after Google and one of the low-cost marketing ideas in India.

Many businesses engage in advertising on YouTube. They get in contact with other YouTubers and enter into a contract where the influencer will talk about its product/service and the number of viewers is the potential customers. Usually, the investment is high, but not always. For a comparatively smaller startup, you can reach out to regional YouTubers that have a considerable number of subscribers, not necessarily in millions, and make them promote your business.

YouTubers upload creative content on the platform, and there are creative ways to sneak in product placement in a very interesting manner. Even a small influencer can lead to a lot of benefits for your business. It is an unarguably cheaper way of advertising than paying high-profile actors to do an ad campaign that airs on TVs. You can even create your own YouTube channel where you talk about your product/services, its benefits, and usage, etc., and make the audience aware of your business.

a) **Tag people (and brands)** on social media: Tagging your loyal customers, brand evangelists, or even neighboring companies and vendors on social media can broaden the organic reach of your business to a new potential audience, help you grow your following, and potentially even attain more clients. You should also encourage your followers to tag your social media handle or business location in their posts.

> **There are things more pressing than becoming excessively wealthy and we in MLM have the money and time freedom to make a difference.**

b) **Use hashtags**: Another free marketing tactic that can broaden your reach is to incorporate hashtags into your social media posts—on Instagram, Twitter, and TikTok for sure but also on Facebook and LinkedIn.

   Broad or trending hashtags can help you reinforce your brand identity, but they should not be the only hashtags you use. More specific hashtags (sort of like long-tail keywords) are good for when you're providing resources or advice. Location-based hashtags are a must if you're a local business. And don't forget custom hashtags! Apply a mix of hashtag types in your posts so they can reach the people for whom they are meant.

c) **Use LinkedIn**: LinkedIn is a major social media site that is often under-utilized. Don't just add network connections and sign out; enter into dialogue with the connections you make, share your blog posts and offers, join and contribute to forums, and share others' quality content.

d) **Start a blog**: One great way to make content a regular part of your marketing efforts is to start a blog. Small businesses use blogging to drive traffic to their website, increase user engagement, improve their online visibility, and strengthen their overall SEO. It's a completely free way to promote your small business online, through tales about your business and useful information your potential clients are seeking out. Blog posts don't have to be long and complex—speak in simple terms, target a different topic with each post, and incorporate the keywords you're targeting into each post in a natural way.

e) **Run informative webinars:** If reaching a potential audience in person doesn't sound like your idea of a good marketing idea, you can always host a webinar. Webinars are a free way to promote your business by providing helpful information to potentially interested customers. Many webinar platforms allow you to broadcast your webinar with just a few button clicks. Make sure to promote your webinar on social media or through an email newsletter one to two weeks before the event and include reminders to registrants so that they don't miss it.

f) **Cloud meetings**: - One of the most obvious but important benefits of video conferencing or cloud meetings is a reduction in commute time. In-person meetings with distributors, customers, and company offices can take up valuable hours of your day. Even an hour-long meeting can quickly eat up an entire morning when accounting for travel time, making it a frustrating and inefficient activity. Efficient multi-city working is achieved by cloud meetings.

The most popular tools in cloud meetings are Zoom and Microsoft Team. They gained popularity as they provide live chat, content sharing, interactive whiteboarding, and many other features to make meetings more productive. Whilst many will argue that there is no substitute for face-to-face meetings, Cloud Meetings can do things that traditional meetings cannot. These meetings can help you train distributors/customers in various locations at the same time, can be used for presenting the product or an opportunity, conduct core group meetings, and many more.

g) **Search Engine Optimization (SEO):** This is one of the cost-effective digital marketing strategies for startups of getting pages to rank higher in Search Engine Result Page (SERPs). In other words, it is a method to grow your business by the efficient and effective use of available resources thereby improving the quality of your website. It is a bit technical but you can take a course on it in order to understand the basics and how it works. SEO is the best way to increase the visibility of traffic to your website.

h) **Develop an email marketing plan**: Email marketing is a great way to get new visitors engaged with your business, as well as to maintain relationships with your existing customers. Though email marketing isn't new, it's still one of—if not the—the most reliable ways to achieve a strong return on your marketing investment. Here's how to ensure that:

- Put thought and creativity into your subject lines.

- Make sure every email has an offer that encourages your readers to take the next step.

- Track your performance to see what copy and offers resonate with your list.

i) **Participate in social events**: Actively volunteering for social events can make your brand look better and people can get to know you better. It's almost like marketing with no budget. If you have a big warehouse or office, giving it out for these social events once in a while can make you popular in no time.

j) **Host classes and events**: Plan an event or a class. Print out flyers and post them on community bulletin boards (libraries, coffee shops, local colleges, and adult ed centers). While most community bulletin boards won't let you post business advertisements, they're often more than happy to post a flyer promoting an educational event or class.

If you can't host an event, attend any local events that you can find that might benefit your business. You never know where you will find your next customer or business partner!

9.8   Get testimonials

Get your downlines to write testimonials or better record video testimonials of how they have benefited from the business or products. People tend to believe in the written rather than verbal word. Include photographs of the downlines to make it even more realistic.

9.9   Combining business and pleasure

When Michael decided to extend his distributorship internationally, he and his wife chose the Philippines, which was a largely untapped market. They traveled to Manila Occasionally and during that time, they were able to see the country which they had always wanted to.

9.10   Public relations

You want visibility in this industry Your Company might have a regular in-house newsletter or magazine. Get one of your downlines to write about you, and get it published in the newsletter. Do the same with local papers and magazines. Offer to write a column if they don't want to write about you e.g. on how to run a home-based business. The article written has a lot more credibility than an advertisement.

PR ideas

A PR tactic worth considering: List the home or contact phone numbers of your top distributors on the back of your card or in any of your brochures. It gives you credibility and makes them feel good. You and your top distributors may not get a lot of calls, but seeing it in writing would impress your prospective recruits.

Low-cost incentive

Other low-cost benefits can be offered to your top downlines: Run a series of seminars to help them manage their life and family better. Or invite health experts to talk to your network. You will benefit from healthy, energetic distributors. As an incentive, invite your downline for dinner or dinner functions e.g. local Rotary Club dinner, where you can use the opportunity to get him to network.

Battery recharge

It pays to recharge not only your own battery but those of your top distributors.

Give a weekend incentive; e.g., sponsor a stay in a suite or a short cruise. Even better would be to plan a group getaway and make it a family affair without any official agenda. Just fun and games.

Surveys

The needs of your downlines may not always be known by you. In such cases, a survey can be useful. Getting constructive feedback requires careful design and administration of questionnaires. You may be surprised by the remarks you get from the downlines. Do you know what incentives will motivate them? If not, find out by asking them what makes them tick.

9.11   Email and social media

Use email and social media to the fullest capacity. The first step is to collect email addresses from all your downlines. If you hear of new ideas or encouragement, you could pass them on to everybody. Your downlines can also do likewise.

Tell it like it was

A good recruiting tool is one that allows you to demonstrate how you lived before you joined the network marketing and how you have evolved your lifestyle. You could do a video of your humble beginnings and the fame and prosperity that network marketing has brought you now. The point is to get your prospect's imagination running. If the prospect sees how it is possible for them, it will propel them to jump in.

Taping your goals

Interview your downlines and ask if they are genuinely serious in the business. Ask them to verbalize their goal. It has been found that if you replay the taped goal, and listen to your own voice regularly, it has a greater and more powerful impact on you to realize your goals. Get your distributors to listen to their own commitments.

9.12   Get to know your downline well

This business is a relationship business and one of the most important relationships you need to foster is that with our top distributors. Get to know him and his family well. Memorize the names of his wife and kids. It seems minor but it can be significant to him. One of the best ways to get to know your downlines well and quickly is to travel with them. Go on joint business trips together.

Repeating the goals

The biggest problem with team goals is that most of the time they're communicated to your team just once, if at all, at the beginning of the year. After that, it's easy to forget that whatever you and everyone else bought, somehow fits into the plan. Get the goals in front of them as often as you can. Repetition will reinforce commitments. The same goes for personal goals. Gerry Robert taught people to write their goals down and then transfer them to another piece of paper every day! It works wonders for me.

MINISTRY OF CONSUMER AFFAIRS, FOOD AND PUBLIC DISTRIBUTION

(Department of Consumer Affairs) NOTIFICATION

New Delhi, the 28th December, 2021

G.S.R. 889(E).—In exercise of the powers conferred by clause (zg) of sub-section (2) of section 101 read with section 94 of the Consumer Protection Act, 2019, the Central Government hereby makes the following rules, namely:-

1. **Short title and commencement.**

(1) These rules may be called the Consumer Protection (Direct Selling) Rules, 2021.

(2) They shall come into force on the date of their publication in the Official Gazette.

2. **Application.**

(1) Save as otherwise expressly provided, these rules shall apply to—

    (a) all goods and services bought or sold through direct selling;

    (b) all models of direct selling;

    (c) all direct selling entities offering goods and services to consumers in India;

(d) all forms of unfair trade practices across all models of direct selling:

Provided that existing direct selling entities shall comply with the provisions of these rules within ninety days from the date of publication of these rules in the Official Gazette;

(2) Notwithstanding anything contained in sub-rule (1), these rules shall also apply to a direct selling entity which is not established in India, but offers goods or services to consumers in India.

3. Definitions.

(1) In these rules, unless the context otherwise requires,—

(a) "Act" means the Consumer Protection Act, 2019 (35 of 2019);

(b) "cooling-off period" means a period of time given to a participant to cancel the agreement he has entered into for participating in the direct selling business without resulting in any breach of contract or levy of penalty;

(c) "direct seller" means a person authorized by a direct selling entity through a legally enforceable written contract to undertake direct selling business on principal to principal basis;

(d) "direct selling entity" means the principal entity which sells or offers to sell goods or services through direct sellers, but does not include an entity which is engaged in a Pyramid Scheme or money circulation scheme;

(f) "money circulation scheme" means the schemes defined in clause (c) of section 2 of the Prize Chits and Money Circulation Schemes (Banning) Act, 1978 (43 of 1978);

(g) "mis-selling" means selling a product or service by misrepresenting in order to successfully complete a sale and includes providing consumers with misleading information about a product or service or omitting key information about a product or providing information that makes the product appear to be something it is not;

(h) "prospect" means a person to whom an offer or a proposal is made by a direct seller to join a direct selling entity;

(i) "Pyramid Scheme" means a multi layered network of subscribers to a scheme formed by subscribers enrolling one or more subscribers in order to receive any benefit, directly or indirectly, as a result of enrolment or action or performance of additional subscribers to the scheme, in which the subscribers enrolling further subscribers occupy a higher position and the enrolled subscribers a lower position, resulting in a multi-layered network of subscribers with successive enrolments:

(j) "saleable", in relation to goods or services, means unused and marketable goods or services which have not expired, and which are not seasonal, discontinued or used for special promotion;

(k) "sensitive personal data" means the sensitive data or information as specified from time to time under section 43A of the Information Technology Act, 2000 (21 of 2000);

(l) "State" includes a Union territory;

(2) Words and expressions used herein and not defined, but defined in the Act shall have the meanings respectively assigned to them in the Act.

4. Mandatory maintenance of records.— Every direct selling entity shall maintain at its registered office, either manually or electronically, all such documents as are required under any law for the time being in force, including the following documents or records, as may be applicable, namely:–

(a) Certificate of Incorporation;

(b) Memorandum of Association and Articles of Association;

(c) Permanent Account Number and Tax Deduction and Collection Account Number;

(d) Goods and Services Tax registration; (e) Goods and Services Tax Returns;

(f) Income Tax Returns;

(g) Balance Sheet, Audit Report and such other relevant reports; (h) Register of direct sellers;

(i) Certificate of Importer-Exporter code (in case of imported goods)

(j) License issued under the Food Safety and Standards Authority of India Act, 2006 (34 of 2006) for the purposes of manufacture or sale of food items;

(k) License and Registration Certificate issued under the Drugs and Cosmetics Act, 1940 (23 of 1940) for the purposes of manufacture or sale of drugs, including Ayurvedic, Siddha and Unani drugs and Homoeopathic Medicines;

(l) Certificate of Registration of Trademark.

5. Obligations of direct selling entity.—

(1) Every direct selling entity shall–

(a) if a company, be incorporated under the Companies Act, 2013 (18 of 2013) or if a partnership firm, be registered under the Partnership Act, 1932 (9 of 1932) or if a limited liability partnership, be registered under the Limited Liability Partnership Act, 2008 (6 of 2009);

(b) have a minimum of one physical location as its registered office within India;

(c) make self-declaration to the effect that it has complied with the provisions of these rules and is not involved in any Pyramid Scheme or money circulation scheme;

(d) maintain proper and updated website with all relevant details of that entity, including the documents or records specified in rule 4, the self-declaration specified in clause (c), contact information which is current and updated, details of its nodal officer, grievance redressal officer, its management, products, product information, price and grievance redressal mechanism for consumers;

(e) own, hold or be the licensee of a trademark, service mark or any other identification mark which identifies that entity with the goods or services to be sold or supplied, but shall not give commissions, bonus or incentives on sale of goods or services of which it is not the owner, holder or licensee of trademark, service mark or other identification marks;

(f) obtain all applicable trade registrations and licenses, including Permanent Account Number and Goods and Services Tax Registration;

(g) get all information provided by it on its website duly certified by a Company Secretary.

    Explanation.—For the purposes of this clause, "Company Secretary" means a person as defined in clause (c) of sub-section (1) of section 2 of the Company Secretaries Act, 1980 (56 of 1980);

(h) have a prior written contract with its direct sellers in order to authorize them to sell or offer to sell its goods or services, and the terms of such agreement shall be just, fair and equitable;

(i) ensure that all its direct sellers have verified identities and physical addresses and issue identity cards and documents only to such direct sellers;

(j) create adequate safeguards to ensure that goods and services offered by its direct sellers conform to applicable laws;

(k) be liable for the grievances arising out of the sale of goods or services by its direct sellers.

(2) Every direct selling entity shall provide the following information on its website in a clear and accessible manner, which shall be displayed prominently to its users, namely:—

(a) registered name of the direct selling entity;

(b) registered address of the direct selling entity and of its branches;

(c) contact details, including e-mail address, fax, land line and mobile numbers of its customer care and grievance redressal officers;

(d) a ticket number for each complaint lodged through which the complainant can track the status of the complaint;

(e) information relating to return, refund, exchange, warranty and guarantee, delivery and shipment, modes of payment, grievance redressal mechanism and such other information which may be required by the consumers to make informed decisions;

(f) information on available payment methods, the security of those payment methods, the fees or charges payable by users, the procedure to cancel regular payments under those methods, charge-back options, if any, and the contact information of the relevant payment service provider;

(g) total price of any goods or service in single figure, along with its break-up price showing all compulsory and voluntary charges, including delivery charges, postage and handling charges, conveyance charges and the applicable tax;

(h) provide correct and complete information at pre-purchase stage to enable buyers to make informed purchase decisions, and such information shall, in addition to the mandatory declarations to be provided under the Legal Metrology (Packaged Commodities) Rules, 2011, contain the following information, namely:—

(i) the name of purchaser and seller;

(ii) description of goods or services;

(iii) quantity of goods or services;

(iv) the estimated delivery date of goods or services;

(v) the process of refund;

(vi) warranty of the goods;

(vii) exchange or replacement of goods in case of it being defective;

(viii) all contractual information required to be disclosed by or under any law for the time being in force.

(3) No direct selling entity shall adopt any unfair trade practice in the course of its business or otherwise, and shall abide by the requirements specified in any law for the time being in force.

(4) All products of a direct selling entity shall comply with the declarations to be made under the Legal Metrology Act, 2009 (1 of 2010).

(5) Every direct selling entity shall store sensitive personal data within the jurisdiction of India, in accordance with the applicable law for the time being in force and shall take appropriate steps to ensure protection of such data provided by a consumer and also ensure adequate safeguards to prevent access or misuse of such data by any unauthorized person.

(6) Every direct selling entity shall, having regard to the number of grievances ordinarily received by such entity from persons in India, establish an adequate grievance redressal mechanism and appoint one or more grievance redressal officers for redressal of consumers' grievances and display the current and updated name, contact details including telephone number, email address and designation of such officer on its website, and the details of its website shall also be prominently printed on the product information sheet or pamphlet.

(7) Every direct selling entity shall ensure that the grievance redressal officer referred to in sub-rule (6) acknowledges the receipt of any consumer complaint within forty-eight working hours of receipt of such complaint and redresses the complaint normally within a period of one month from the date of receipt of the complaint and in case of delay of more than a month, reasons for the delay, and the actions taken on the complaint, are informed to the complainant in writing.

(8) Every direct selling entity shall appoint a nodal officer who shall be responsible for ensuring compliance with the provisions of the Act and the rules made thereunder, and to ensure compliance with any order, or requisition, made in accordance with the provisions of any other law for the time being in force or the rules made thereunder.

(9) Every direct selling entity shall establish a mechanism for filing of complaints by consumers through its offices or branches or direct sellers, either in person or through post, telephone, e-mail or website.

(10) Every direct selling entity shall maintain a record of all its direct sellers, including their identity proof, address proof, e-mail and such other contact information.

(11) Every direct selling entity shall, on the request in writing made by a consumer after the purchase of any goods or services, provide him with the information regarding any direct seller from whom such consumer has made a purchase, and such information shall include the name, address, e-mail, contact number and any other information which is necessary for making communication with such direct seller for effective dispute resolution.

(12)Every direct selling entity shall ensure that the advertisements for marketing of goods or services are consistent with the actual characteristics, access and usage conditions of such goods or services.

(13)No direct selling entity shall, directly or indirectly, falsely represent itself as a consumer and post reviews about its goods or services or misrepresent the quality or features of any of its goods or services.

(14)A direct selling entity which explicitly or implicitly vouches for the authenticity of the goods or services sold, or guarantees that such goods or services are authentic, shall bear the liability in any action related to the authenticity of such goods or services.

(15)Notwithstanding the distribution system adopted by it, a direct selling entity shall monitor the practices adopted by its direct sellers and ensure compliance with these rules by means of legally binding contract with such direct sellers.

(16)Every direct selling entity shall maintain a record of relevant information allowing for the identification of all direct sellers who have been delisted by the direct selling entity and such list shall be publicly shared on its website.

(17)Every direct selling entity shall become a partner in the convergence process of the National Consumer Helpline of the Central Government.

6. Obligations of direct seller.

(1) Every direct seller shall—

   (a) have a prior written contract with the direct selling entity for undertaking sale of, or offer to sell, any goods or services of such entity;

   (b) at the initiation of any sale representation, truthfully and clearly identify himself, disclose the identity of the direct selling entity, the address of place of business, the nature of goods or services sold and the purpose of such solicitation to the prospect;

   (c) make an offer to the prospect providing accurate and complete information, demonstration of goods and services, prices, credit terms, terms of payment, return, exchange, refund policy, return policy, terms of guarantee and after-sale service;

(d) provide an order form to the consumer at or prior to the time of the initial sale, which shall identify the direct selling entity and the direct seller and shall contain the name, address, registration number or enrollment number, identity proof and contact number of the direct seller, complete description of the goods or services to be supplied, the country of origin of the goods, the order date, the total amount to be paid by the consumer, the time and place for inspection of the sample and delivery of goods, consumer's rights to cancel the order or to return the product in saleable condition and avail full refund on sums paid and complete details regarding the complaint redressal mechanism of the direct selling entity;

(e) obtain goods and service tax registration, Permanent Account Number registration, all applicable trade registrations and licenses and comply with the requirements of applicable laws, rules and regulations for sale of a product;

(f) ensure that actual product delivered to the buyer matches with the description of the product given;

(g) take appropriate steps to ensure the protection of all sensitive personal information provided by the consumer in accordance with the applicable laws for the time being in force and ensure adequate safeguards to prevent access to, or misuse of, data by unauthorized persons.

(2) A direct seller shall not—

(a) visit a consumer's premises without identity card and prior appointment or approval;

(b) provide any literature to a prospect, which has not been approved by the direct selling entity;

(c) require a prospect to purchase any literature or sales demonstration equipment;

(d) in pursuance of a sale, make any claim that is not consistent with claims authorized by the direct selling entity.

7. Duties of direct selling entity and direct seller. —Subject to the provisions of Chapter VI of the Act, relating to Product Liability, the following shall be the duties of direct selling entity and direct seller, as may be applicable, namely:—

(i) Every direct selling entity and every direct seller shall ensure that—

    (a) the terms of the offer are clear, so as to enable the consumer to know the exact nature of offer being made and the commitment involved in placing any order;

    (b) the presentations and other representations used in direct selling shall not contain any product description, claim, illustration or other element which, directly or by implication, is likely to mislead the consumer;

    (c) the explanation and demonstration of the goods or services offered are accurate and complete, particularly with regard to price and, if applicable, to credit conditions, terms of payment, cooling-off periods or right to return, terms of guarantee, after-sales service and delivery;

    (d) the descriptions, claims, illustrations or other elements relating to verifiable facts are capable of substantiation;

    (e) any misleading, deceptive or unfair trade practices are not used;

    (f) direct selling is not represented to the consumer as being a form of market research;

    (g) the promotional literature, advertisement or mail contain the name and address or telephone number of the direct selling company, and include the mobile number of the direct seller;

    (h) direct selling shall not state or imply that a guarantee, warranty or other expression having substantially the same meaning, offers to the consumer any rights in additional to those provided by law, when it does not;

    (i) the terms of any guarantee or warranty, including the name and address of the guarantor, shall be easily available to the consumer and limitations on consumer rights or remedies, where permitted by law, shall be clear and conspicuous;

(j) the remedial action open to the consumer shall be clearly set out in the order form or other accompanying literature provided with the goods or service;

(k) the presentation of the offer does not contain or refer to any testimonial, endorsement or supportive documentation unless it is genuine, verifiable and relevant;

(l) when after-sales service is offered, details of the service are included in the guarantee or stated elsewhere in the offer and if the consumer accepts the offer, information shall be given on how the consumer can activate the service and communicate with the service agent;

(m) products, including, where applicable, samples, are suitably packaged for delivery to the consumer and for possible return, in compliance with the appropriate health and safety standards;

(n) unless otherwise stipulated in the offer, orders shall be fulfilled within the delivery date proposed to the consumer at the time of purchase and the consumer shall be informed of any undue delay as soon as it becomes apparent or comes within the knowledge of the direct selling entity or the concerned direct seller;

(o) in cases of delay under clause (n), any request for cancellation of the order by the consumer shall be granted, irrespective of whether the consumer has been informed of the delay, and the deposit, if any, shall be refunded as per the cancellation terms proposed to the consumer at the time of purchase, and if it is not possible to prevent delivery, the consumer shall be informed of the right to return the product at the direct selling company's or the direct seller's cost as per the procedure for return of the goods proposed to the consumer at the time of purchase;

(p) right of return offered by that entity shall be in writing;

(q) whether payment for the offer is on an immediate sale or installment basis, the price and terms of payment shall be clearly stated in the offer together with the nature of any additional charges such as postage, handling and taxes and, whenever possible, the amounts of such charges;

(r) in the case of sales by installment, the credit terms, including the amount of any deposit or payment on account, the number, amount and periodicity of such installments and the total price compared with the immediate selling price, if any, shall be clearly shown in the offer;

(s) any information needed by the consumer to understand the cost, interest and terms of any other form of credit is provided either in the offer or when the credit is offered;

(t) unless the duration of the offer and the price are clearly stated in the offer, prices shall be maintained for a reasonable period of time;

(u) the procedure for payment and debt collection shall be determined in writing before any contract is signed and it shall be such as to avoid undue inconvenience to the consumer, making due allowance for delays outside the consumer's control;

(v) the provisions of the Legal Metrology Act, 2009 (1 of 2010) and the rules framed thereunder shall be followed.

(ii) A direct selling entity or direct seller shall not—

(a) indulge in fraudulent activities or sales and shall take reasonable steps to ensure that participants do not indulge in false or misleading representations or any other form of fraud, coercion, harassment, or unconscionable or unlawful means;

(b) engage in, or cause or permit, any conduct that is misleading or likely to mislead with regard to any material particulars relating to its direct selling business, or to the goods or services being sold by itself or by the direct seller;

(c) indulge in mis-selling of products or services to consumers;

(d) use, or cause or permit to be used, any fraudulent, coercive, unconscionable or unlawful means, or cause harassment, for promoting its direct selling business, or for sale of its goods or services;

(e) refuse to take back spurious goods or deficient services and refund the consideration paid for goods and services provided;

(f) charge any entry fee or subscription fee.

(iii) A direct selling entity and a direct seller shall comply with the requirements of all relevant laws, including payment of taxes and deductions thereunder.

(iv) A direct selling entity and a direct seller shall not induce consumers to make a purchase based upon the representation that they can reduce or recover the price by referring prospective customers to the direct sellers for similar purchases.

8. Persons not to be engaged in the business of direct selling.— No person who is convicted, or bankrupt during the last five years prior to his association with the business of direct selling, or a person of unsound mind, shall be engaged in the business of direct selling.

   Explanation.—For the purpose of this rule, the term 'Bankrupt' shall have the same meaning as assigned to it in clause (3) of section 79 of the Insolvency and Bankruptcy Code, 2016 (31 of 2016).

9. **Application of e-commerce rules.**— The direct sellers as well as the direct selling entities using e-commerce platforms for sale shall comply with the requirements of the Consumer Protection (e-Commerce) Rules, 2020.

10. Prohibition of Pyramid Scheme and money circulation scheme.—No direct selling entity or direct seller shall—

    (a) promote a Pyramid Scheme or enroll any person to such scheme or participate in such arrangement in any manner whatsoever in the garb of doing direct selling business;

    (b) participate in money circulation scheme in the garb of doing direct selling business.

11. **Monitoring by State Government.**— For ensuring compliance of these rules by direct selling entity and direct sellers, every State Government shall set up a mechanism to monitor or supervise the activities of direct sellers and direct selling entity.

12. Inconsistencies in laws.— Where any regulation made under the Reserve Bank of India Act, 1934 (2 of 1934) is applicable to a direct selling entity governed under these rules, the provisions of such

regulations shall prevail over the provisions of these rules to the extent of inconsistency.

13. Contravention of rules.— The provisions of the Act shall apply for any contravention of these rules.

[F. No. J-10/9/2018-CPU] ANUPAM MISHRA, Jt. Secy.

Uploaded by Dte. of Printing at Government of India Press, Ring Road, Mayapuri, New Delhi-110064

and Published by the Controller of Publications, Delhi-110054.

MANOJ KUMAR

Digitally signed by Manoj Kumar Verma

Date: 2021.12.28, 22:59:57, +05'30'